Explore

the Seashore of South Africa

Margo Branch

CAMBRIDGE
UNIVERSITY PRESS

PUBLISHED BY THE PRESS SYNDICATE OF THE UNIVERSITY OF CAMBRIDGE
The Pitt Building, Trumpington Street, Cambridge CB2 1RP, United Kingdom

CAMBRIDGE UNIVERSITY PRESS
The Edinburgh Building, Cambridge CB2 2RU, United Kingdom
40 West 20th Street, New York, NY 10011–4211, USA
10 Stamford Road, Oakleigh, Melbourne 3166, Australia
1 The Moorings, Victoria and Alfred Waterfront, Cape Town 8001, South Africa

Text and illustrations © Margo Branch
Photographs © George Branch
Design and typesetting Angela Ashton

First published by Struik Publishers, Cape Town, 1987
This edition first published by Cambridge University Press, 1998

Typeset in Concorde and Meta

ISBN 0 521 58554 6

Contents

Introduction

More than two thirds of the earth's surface is covered with water and almost all of this is salty sea water. An amazing variety of animals live in the sea but the richest and most fascinating life occurs on the seashore. For where the land and sea meet there are many different habitats influenced by tides, currents, wind, waves and the sun.

This book will take you on an adventure to discover first hand the wonderful creatures that inhabit the coast of South Africa. This rugged shore is bathed by two oceans. The warm Indian Ocean to the east with many bright tropical animals and the cold Atlantic Ocean to the west with vast kelp forests and shoals of silver fish. You will search the sandy beaches and rocky shores, look under stones and in pools for crabs, seaweeds and shells and lift your eyes to watch dolphins leap and seagulls soar. You will learn about red tides caused by tiny plankton and huge whales, the biggest animals on earth and the interesting plants and creatures in between. They depend on one another and belong to finely balanced ecosystems which we must help to conserve.

Come and explore.

Contrasting life in two oceans

South Africa has a sheer unprotected coast bathed by the Indian Ocean to the east and the Atlantic Ocean to the west. There are three main coastal zones (east, west and south) that have different sea temperatures resulting in different marine communities and climates on land. Cape Agulhas is the southern-most tip of Africa. Cape Point is the division between the south and west coasts, with distinct sea life and different sea temperatures on either side of the Cape Peninsula.

West coast (9–15 °C)

The Benguela Current flows northwards along the west coast, bringing cold water from the south. When a south-easterly wind blows surface water offshore, icy cold water wells up to replace it. This brings nutrients up from the sea floor. Plant plankton and kelp forests grow in this rich water and provide a vast food supply. This food supports enormous numbers of animals, but only a few different species. These mainly include silver schooling fish, mussels, limpets and rock lobsters. Many people make a living by harvesting kelp, fish and shellfish.

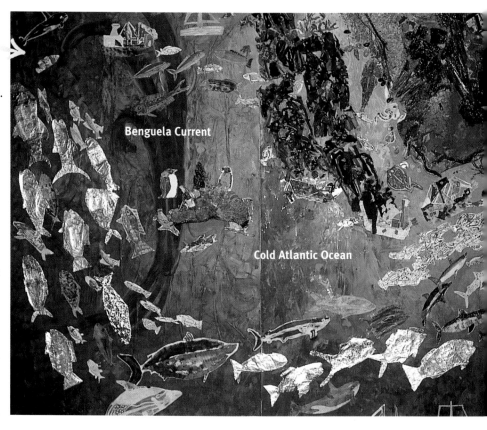

Benguela Current

Cold Atlantic Ocean

things to do

Make a mural that shows some of the contrasting marine life that lives in the two oceans off South Africa's east and west coasts:

Cut out or model a map of South Africa. Paint the sea deep blue on the warm east coast and a brilliant turquoise on the colder west coast. Also show the direction of the currents.

East coast: make lots of small colourful tropical fish using paint, pencils and coloured paper. Try using potato-cut prints for colourful coral and add a few crabs with folded paper legs.

West coast: cut out kelp plants from material or coloured plastic sheets. Make large silver fish by covering a cardboard fish shape with tin foil. Press in scales, eyes and other textures using a teaspoon, tooth-pick or pen lid. Rub shoe polish over the fish so that the scales stand out, and then polish up the shiny highlights. Add fishing boats made from paper, material and match sticks.

South coast: create a sardine run by printing shoals of sardines, followed by larger silver fish, dolphins and sharks.

Marine reserves

One of the best ways for a country to conserve marine life is to set aside marine reserves. These provide a safe place where plants and animals can breed and grow. Active animals and the larvae of sedentary animals can also move out of a reserve and stock adjacent areas.

If marine reserves are to be successful they must:

1 Be large enough.
2 Represent all the major coastal regions and include a variety of habitats. These could be sandy and rocky shorelines, sheltered and exposed areas or lagoons and estuaries.
3 Access to reserves must be controlled and poaching stopped.
4 They must be areas of benefit to marine life and to all people for education, financial income and recreation.
5 Everyone has a responsibility to care for the reserve and use it wisely. This includes the government, visitors and local communities.

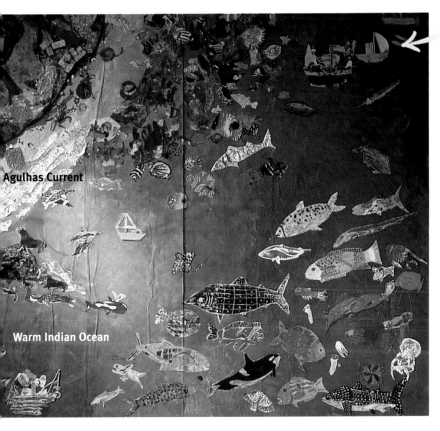

Agulhas Current

Warm Indian Ocean

This mural was prepared by over 100 children from Cape Town

East coast (22 – 27 °C)

The powerful Agulhas Current flows southwards along the east coast bringing warm clear water from the tropics with low levels of nutrients and very little plant plankton. The seaweeds are small and contain lime or chemicals to deter grazers. The animals that feed on the seaweed must compete for the scarce food. Many of the animals are carnivorous instead and feed on one another. So it is a dangerous environment in which to live.

The competition has led to the development of many different species, with some remarkable adaptations and habits. But there are only a few individuals of each type. There are corals, crabs, lots of small brightly coloured fish and many large predators. The animals often have poisonous spines and the shells are thick and ridged for defence.

Holiday-makers flock to the east coast where the water is warm and line fishing is popular.

South coast (16 – 20 °C)

The south coast is an intermediate region where the currents vary seasonally. There are seaweeds but no kelps. In winter, sardines migrate through this region to spawn on the east coast and are followed by larger fish like dolphins and sharks. Whales visit in winter. This is also a popular holiday region.

Floaters

After a storm different types of floating animals often wash up on the beach. Look out for the bluebottle, the by-the-wind sailor and the bubble-raft shell.

things to do

Collect animals washed up after a storm. Float them in a pool or clear container of sea water. Why are they blue or colourless?

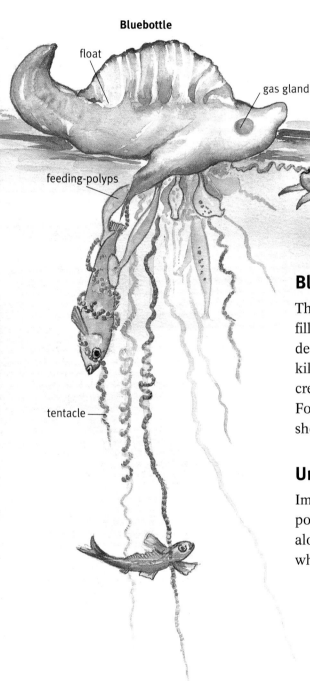

Bluebottle

float

gas gland

feeding-polyps

Bubble-raft shell

tentacle

A fish called **Nomeus** is not stung by the bluebottle's long tentacles, where it shelters unharmed and safe from larger fish

Bluebottles

The bluebottle (sometimes called a Portuguese man-o'-war) has a gas-filled balloon which helps it float on the sea. Beneath its float it trails deadly stinging tentacles. The stings on these tentacles paralyse and kill the fish on which the bluebottle feeds. The bluebottle is not a single creature but a colony of animals called polyps each with different uses. For example, the tentacle-polyps, which may be over 10 metres long, shorten and coil up to carry the food to the feeding-polyps.

Unusual food

Imagine eating the stinging tentacles of a bluebottle! Despite the powerful sting, this is what some sea slugs and snails do as they float alongside the bluebottle. One such sea snail, the bubble-raft shell, which makes a raft of bubbles to help it float, feeds on the bluebottle.

things to do

Float a bubble-raft shell next to a bluebottle. Watch to see if it feeds on the bluebottle or makes new bubbles for the raft. Look at the purple dye the bubble-raft shell produces.

Second-hand stings

The sea swallow is a beautiful sea slug about two centimetres long. Its body spreads like wings to help it float on the sea. It uses the stings of the bluebottle that it feeds on in an unusual way. The stinging cells travel through the gut of the sea swallow without causing any damage. They then pass to the surface of the slug's skin where they are used as second-hand stinging weapons.

Look out for sea swallows – they are small but quite common in summer.

By-the-wind sailor

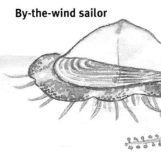

Porpita

Rafts to float

The by-the-wind sailor has a delicate air-filled raft with a sail above it and short stinging tentacles and feeding-polyps beneath the raft. The circular floating raft of porpita lacks a sail but has beautifully branched tentacles. Their stings are not harmful to humans.

Box jellyfish

things to do

If you can find a bluebottle, look for the gland that makes the gas which fills the float. Look to see how the bluebottle wets its float.

If you are stung by a bluebottle, don't rub the painful area with sand or wash it in fresh water. Instead, remove any pieces of tentacle and wash your skin carefully with salty water. Treat it with vinegar and ice or soak in very hot water to relieve the pain. Severe cases are rare but should be treated by a doctor.

Common root mouth jellyfish up to 1.5m wide

Jellyfish

The transparent jellyfish is almost invisible to both its enemies and the tiny creatures on which it feeds. It swims by contracting and expanding its umbrella-like bell. In the centre of the bell is the mouth surrounded by frilly lips. There are four pouches underneath the bell where the eggs are formed. Most jellyfish are harmless to humans. The box jellyfish, however, has four long tentacles and gives a venomous sting. It is related to the deadly Australian jellyfish, the sea wasp.

Red banded jellyfish feeds on plankton and small fish

Sandy shore beach cleaners

Although a sandy beach looks empty there are many small creatures hidden away in the sand, safe from the sun and the birds. They clean up what the sea washes onto the beach.

Plough shells eating a bluebottle

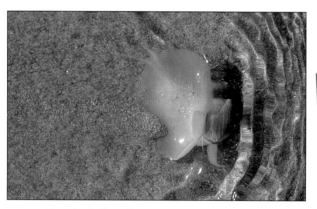

Plough shell surfing

Plough shells

Plough shells feed on dead or dying animals washed up on the beach. They crawl out of the sand at low tide, pump up their large feet and surf up the shore with the waves, landing at the water line along with floaters like bluebottles, on which they feed. Plough shells are able to taste minuscule amounts of substances given off by animals, that have been dissolved in the water. This means they can sense exactly where dead animals are and plough their way straight towards them. However, if they taste a live shark or ray in the water nearby, they burrow quickly into the sand to escape. As high tide approaches they bury themselves so that they can't be stranded high and dry by a large wave.

things to do

Watch plough shells surfing, ploughing and digging. Pick one up and prod it gently. How does it shrink its foot so that it can tuck itself away inside its shell?

White mussels

The white mussel is usually hidden in the sand. It has two tubes called siphons which it sticks into the water above. Water containing minute floating plants called plankton is sucked into the shell through one siphon. Having collected the plankton, the filtered water is then pumped out through the second siphon. Fish sometimes nip the ends off the siphons if they are not pulled inside quickly enough. Small mussels move up and down the shore with the tide.

things to do

Dig up some white mussels. Place them in a bucket filled with sand and water and watch them. Look carefully at the top of the siphon and see how sand is kept out.

siphon

White mussels

Sandy shore birds

Sand plovers feast on sand-hoppers. These little birds seem to twinkle over the sand on their dainty feet. They use their pointed beaks to probe for food. The eggs and the chicks are so well camouflaged that you could easily step on them by mistake. Scavenging seagulls also help to keep the beach clean.

things to do

Watch a sand plover. Can you find its open nest on the sand? Look above the high tide level and follow the bird's footprints to areas behind bits of log or debris. Don't disturb the nest.

Black-backed seagulls eating shells

Sand plover

Night-time gang

After dark, a gang of tiny beach cleaners gets to work. Sand-hoppers and sea lice patiently chew up mountains of kelp and other seaweed. There can be up to 25 000 sand-hoppers in an area the size of a towel. During the day they hide where it is cool and damp. They come out only when it is night time and the tide is low. They have an internal biological clock to keep them on time.

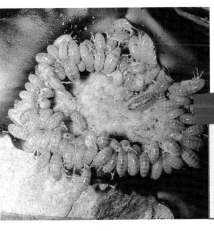

things to do

Lift up a piece of kelp and scratch in the sand underneath – what lives there?

At low tide one night, use a torch to look for the 'clean-up gang'.

Kelp

A group of sand-hoppers and a sea louse seen at night with a torch

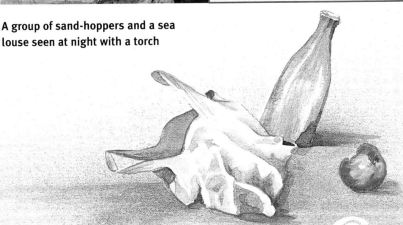

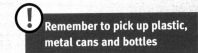
Remember to pick up plastic, metal cans and bottles

Be a crab detective

Crabs have hard protective shells, so they can live successfully in all sorts of places. The shell, which is really an outer skeleton, has joints to allow the legs to bend so that a crab can walk, swim, climb and dig. True crabs have a small, jointed tail folded under the chest. Eggs are attached to the female's tail and look like bunches of tiny red berries.

things to do

Be a crab detective. Inspect crabs for clues and work out how they live. Look at their limbs. Can you imagine why crabs run sideways?

The male **fiddler crab** waves its large coloured nipper to attract a mate. They live in mangrove swamps

Crabs grow out of their shells

As crabs grow they get too big for their shells and must moult. The shell splits and the crab climbs out, leaving behind a perfect shell. After moulting, the soft crab blows itself up with water to expand its body for the new shell. When the new shell is formed and has hardened it is a few sizes bigger. For the few days that the shell is soft, the crab cannot run and is in great danger of being eaten by birds, squid and fish.

things to do

Search the beach for crab shells: remember they are not dead crabs but shells that have been left behind. Can you tell from the clues which crabs have moulted recently and live hidden nearby?

Swimmers

The back legs of the swimming crab are paddle-shaped for swimming. When the crab sinks to the floor of the sea, it also uses the paddles to flick sand over its flat body to hide itself. Fine hairs widen the paddles for swimming and hairs on the body keep sand out of the gill chambers. The body is sandy coloured with red spots. Sharp spines on the edge of the shell and strong nippers protect the crab against attack. The nippers are powerful enough to break open the plough shells and white mussels on which it feeds. So if you see swimming crabs brought in by the trek nets, be careful!

Mole crab gathering food with its feathery feelers

Swimming crab eating a plough shell

Ghost crab

Ghosts

During the day the ghost crab stays cool, moist and safe in its burrow beneath the sand. At dusk it creeps out. It hoists its eyes, which are stalked for long distance vision, and scurries off to collect food washed up by the sea. It uses its strong nippers to crush shells and tear up food. It can sprint over the sand on its long, pointed legs and can vanish sideways down its burrow, like a ghost. Its eyes fold into special grooves and its box-shaped body fits easily into the burrow. One large nipper guards the entrance. Water can be stored in gill chambers at the side of the body so that the crab can breathe out of water during low tide.

things to do

If you are in KwaZulu-Natal, you can watch ghost crabs at dusk. As they are very shy, you may need binoculars.

A surfing crab

The barrel-shaped mole crab cannot walk. Instead it is rolled up and down the beach by the waves. The mole crab's front legs are like spades and are used to dig itself backwards into the sand. The back legs are long and thin and end in small nippers which reach inside the gill chambers to remove sand from the gills. It has long feelers with a fringe of hairs which are held in the water like a net to trap small particles of food. The feelers then curl under the mouth parts which remove the food particles.

things to do

Try and catch a mole crab by holding a net in the breakers at the water's edge in KwaZulu-Natal.

Mole crab surfing

Masters of swimming and colour change

The cuttlefish and the squid are two of the most amazing animals in the sea. Unlike their relatives the snails, they can swim extremely quickly to escape attack. Squids are among the largest invertebrates (animals without backbones) in the sea.

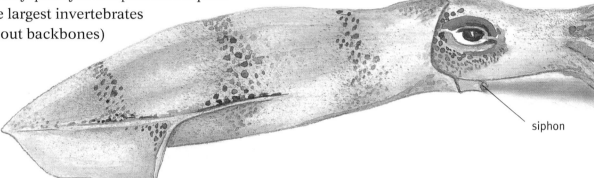

Squid

siphon

Giant deep-sea squid can be over 15 metres long, and sucker marks as big as saucers have been found on whales.

A floating shell

You will often find ramshorn shells washed up on the beach. They are the internal shells of a deep-sea animal called a spirula which floats along with its head down. The internal shell provides it with buoyancy.

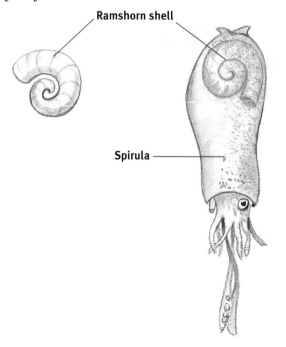

Ramshorn shell

Spirula

Internal surf board

The cuttlefish has a flat internal shell shaped like a surf board. The shell is very light and filled with air spaces which helps it float. The squid has only a thin horny internal shell. Squid and cuttlefish swim slowly by gently rippling the flat fins down each side of the body. However, when they need to escape, they squirt water out of their siphons to jet propel themselves backwards at great speed.

things to do

Look for white cuttlefish shells washed up on the beach. People give these to budgies as the calcium they contain will build strong bones.

Black **cuttlefish eggs** are fastened by loops to seaweeds

Survival strategies

To confuse their enemies while they escape, squid and cuttlefish squirt a cloud of ink into the water. The ink's rich brown colour used in the illustration below is called sepia, which is the scientific name for the cuttlefish. In the past it was made from cuttlefish ink. Squid and cuttlefish can instantly change colour to match the background. Their stripes ripple like the water that passes over them. They also use vivid colour changes to attract their mates.

things to do

Look for squid when the fishers haul in their nets.

ink

Food chain

Squid and cuttlefish have eight arms and two long tentacles with suckers around their mouths. They use these to capture shrimps, crabs and small fish. Squid move in large shoals and are, themselves, an important food for whales, seals, fishes and dolphins. They are a valuable catch for the fishing industry and are sold as a popular seafood known as calamari.

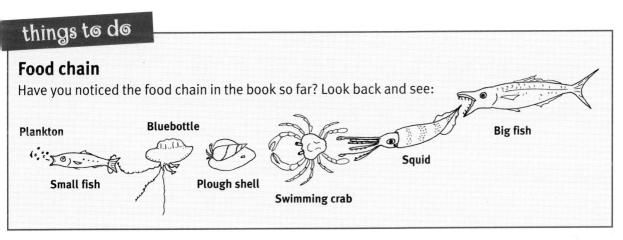

things to do

Food chain
Have you noticed the food chain in the book so far? Look back and see:

Plankton — Small fish — Bluebottle — Plough shell — Swimming crab — Squid — Big fish

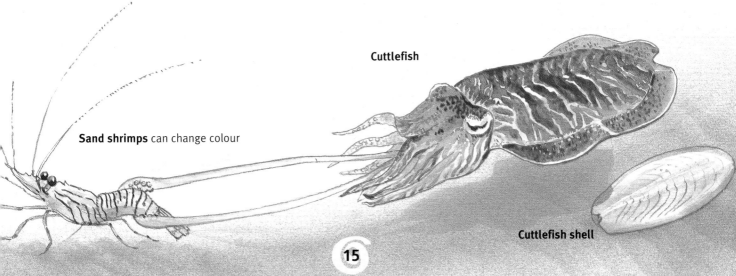

Sand shrimps can change colour

Cuttlefish

Cuttlefish shell

The octopus and the paper nautilus

The octopus and its relatives the paper nautilus, squid, cuttlefish and ramshorn shell, all belong to a group of animals called the cephalopods. This name was chosen from the Greek words for 'head' and 'foot' because most of the animal is made up of a large head and a 'foot' which is divided into eight or ten long arms that surround the mouth.

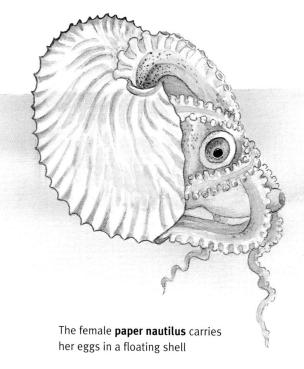

The female **paper nautilus** carries her eggs in a floating shell

Cephalopods – swimming molluscs

It is surprising to learn that the cephalopods are relatives of snails and sea slugs, and are all molluscs (see page 18). The cephalopods have left the sea floor and can swim by squirting water out of their bodies. The cuttlefish, paper nautilus and ramshorn also use their gas-filled shells for buoyancy.

Because they are active, cephalopods have large brains to coordinate their movements. They use their well developed eyes and arms with suckers to find and capture prey. The body is a muscular bag filled with organs and a cavity for the gills. Water is sucked into the cavity through a tube and flows over the gills. In the gills oxygen from the water passes into the blood and the waste gas is removed, so cephalopods breath like fishes do. Unlike fish though, the cephalopods have blue blood running in their veins.

Paper nautilus

The paper nautilus looks like a pale octopus riding in one of the most beautiful and highly-prized shells in the ocean. Only the female builds a shell. She is joined there by a tiny male. After they have mated, she lays thousands of eggs, which stick to the inside of the shell. As they float along, she cares for the eggs by blowing water over them to give them oxygen. The nautilus eats fishes and other small animals.

things to do

To find a paper nautilus shell try and be the first on the beach after a windy night in autumn. You may have to look while it is still dark, before the gulls and shell collectors arrive.

The clever octopus

The octopus is probably the cleverest of all the invertebrates. It learns quickly and easily to recognise shapes and colours. It has wonderful eyes that are very like ours and it has a good sense of balance. The octopus lives in pools and glides over the rocks on its eight suckered arms, feeling along ledges and cracks for hidden food such as shells and crabs. After it grabs an unsuspecting crab and bites it with a powerful beak, the crab is killed by the octopus's poisonous saliva. When angry or in danger, an octopus can change colour instantly. If threatened it can squeeze through spaces as small as its eye or swim rapidly and escape behind an inky smoke screen. One of its main enemies is the moray eel (see page 33).

A good mother

When octopuses mate, the male uses a special long arm to place packets of sperm in the female's mantle cavity. There the sperm fertilises her eggs. The female lays thousands of eggs and they hang like bunches of tiny pale grapes from the wall of the cave where she lives. She is a good mother, protecting her eggs, blowing water over them and keeping them clean. The tiny, transparent youngsters hatch after about 40 days. They grow very quickly and are adult within a year.

things to do

The octopus's lair often has piles of shells and stones near the entrance. Dangle something orange nearby. The octopus may think it is a crab and be lured into the open. But the octopus is not easily fooled!

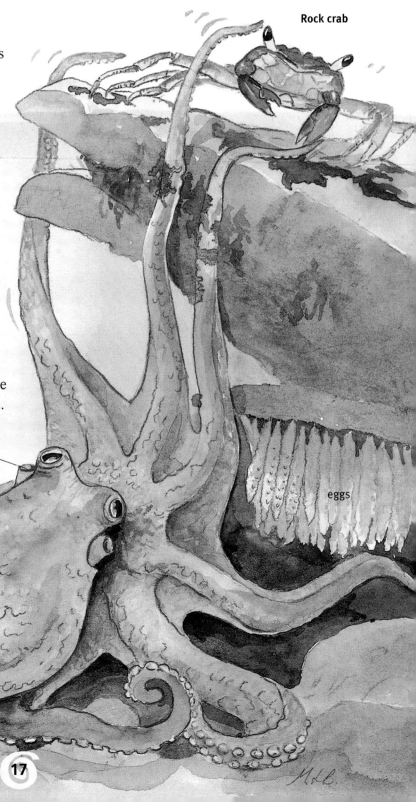

Rock crab

siphon

eggs

Octopus

17

Shells

It is fun collecting shells that wash up on the beach. They often have beautiful colours and shapes and will remind you of your visit to the seashore.

Chitons

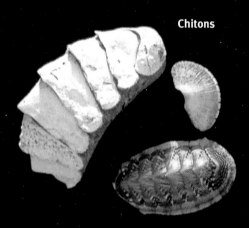

Molluscs

Most shells are made by molluscs. Molluscs are soft-bodied animals like snails and slugs and they usually have a head, a foot and a hump containing body organs. A special skirt of skin, called the mantle, covers the animal and encloses the gills. The shell is made of lime; the inside glistens with beautiful mother-of-pearl but the outside layer is furry or horny and can be pealed off. Colour taken from the food is used to pattern the shell and so some shells look and smell like the seaweeds on which they live.

Sort the shells you collect into the groups shown on this page:

A Chitons are the coat-of-mail shells with eight overlapping shell plates and a tough leathery foot. Some of their shell plates look like a set of false teeth.

B Bivalves have two shells that fit together tightly. They have no head and filter particles of food out of the water.

C Ear shells are ear-shaped with a wide opening.

D Limpets are flat, cone-shaped shells with a wide opening.

E Winkles are coiled shells with a round opening. There are many different types and they eat plant material.

Bivalves

Ear shells

Limpets

F Cowries are shiny egg-shaped shells with long narrow openings.

G Whelks have an oval opening with a notch or long groove and are usually pointed and spiralled. They feed on dead or live animals and have a tube that sticks out through the groove in the shell to taste the water for any food. There are many different types of whelks.

H Bubble shells are the very fragile shells that belong to the few sea slugs that have shells (see page 40).

I Cephalopods include the octopus, which has no shell; the ramshorn shell, the cuttlefish and the paper nautilus, which do have shells.

things to do

Keep your shells labelled, noting where and when you collected them. You can add their names later when you know them.

Try to visit a museum which has a shell collection. Compare shells that have been collected from different parts of the country. Which shells live in the warm waters of KwaZulu-Natal? Which prefer the cold west coast?

Try and find living shells and watch what they do. Some sit on the open rocks, but others hide under stones and seaweeds or dig in the sand.

Cephalopods

Bubble shells

Whelks

Winkles

Cowries

The rocky shore and tides

Every day and night there is a high tide when the water rises high on the shore. Six hours later, at low tide, the water has receded, leaving the intertidal marine life exposed.

Spring and neap tides

Every two weeks there are extra high and extra low tides known as spring tides. Low spring tide is the best time to visit the shore because many exciting animals have been uncovered. But how can we tell when the different tides will occur?

What causes tides?

Tides are caused by the gravitational pull of the moon and the sun. At new moon and full moon, the sun and the moon pull together and cause the very high and very low spring tides.

In South Africa, the low spring tides are at about nine o'clock in the morning and evening. Each day the tides will occur about 50 minutes later, so that after a week the low tide is in the afternoon. At this time we see a half moon and, because the sun and the moon are pulling in different directions, the tides are neither very high nor very low and are called neap tides.

things to do

Keep a record of the times of high and low tide for a week or a month and see how they change.

Look at how the phases of the moon affect the time and height of the tide.

Find out the times of the tides from the weather bulletin in the newspaper. See if you can predict the time of low tide for your next visit to the beach.

Which animals live at which tide levels?

Different animals live in distinct zones at different tide levels. They can indicate to us how high or low the tide is at a particular time. For example, if the water reaches to the barnacle zone we know it is mid-tide.

High tide level

If you explore a rocky shore at high tide, the only live shells you are likely to find are hundreds of tiny littorina shells. There are so many that they seem to litter the rocks! Hardy lichens form beautiful coloured crusts on the rocks and are the only source of food. A lichen is a partnership between a plant and a fungus.

Mid-tide level

When the tide goes out other creatures are uncovered. At mid-tide there are plenty of barnacles making the rocks rough to walk on. There are also limpets and winkles. On the east coast near Durban you can see oysters cemented to the rocks. When the water drops lower, look for mussels, worm tubes, sponges and spiny sea urchins. If you are in the Western Cape, be careful, as there are many slippery seaweeds. And in KwaZulu-Natal take care on the green anemone-like zoanthids.

Low tide level

At low tide you can see many more seaweeds of different types. Some are really beautiful and their purples, blues and greens sparkle in the sun. Others, called corallines, are hard and jointed. Many tiny creatures live among the seaweeds. On the South coast, look for the solid band of pear limpets. Red bait, animals which only become exposed at low spring tide, are sometimes called sea-squirts. Watch them squirt water as they contract their bodies. Look out for big waves when the tide rises again.

Compare the intertidal animals and plants on the west coast near Cape Town (left picture) with those on the east coast near Durban (right pictures). How do they compare with the animals and plants on the rocks where you live?

Intertidal zones on a granite boulder on the west coast near Cape Town

Intertidal zones on an east coast shore near Durban

High spring tide – littorina

High neap tide – barnacles

Mid-tide – seaweeds and barnacles

Low neap tide – mixed community, red bait

Low spring tide

Three kinds of high-shore littorina

A crab shelters amongst oysters at mid-tide level

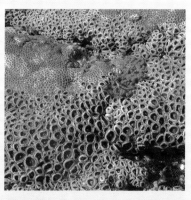

Slippery zoanthids and a bright red sponge at mid-tide level

Brightly coloured seaweeds on the low shore near Durban. Can you spot the three animals hiding in the seaweed?

west

east

Living in a harsh environment

Animals living on the rocks have many problems. When they are out of water during low tide on a hot, windy day, they are in danger of roasting or drying out. At high tide, rough waves can damage them or wash them away. Active animals can escape from danger and hardship, but slower creatures such as snails, barnacles and worms find protection in the hard shells or tubes in which they live.

High and dry

Only animals and plants that are really tough can live at the top of the shore. The littorina shells live highest on the shore and can be out of water for many hours. They crawl into cool cracks and cluster together to shade one another and save moisture. If it is too hot to stand on the rocks, they hang from threads of dried slime and seal up the openings to their shells. Although the waves are not strong high on the shore, food is in short supply. Littorina feed on the thin, black lichen that coats the rocks. It is no wonder that they are small and grow slowly in such a harsh environment.

Tiny, hardy littorina

things to do

Visit the same rocks when it is hot or cool and moist, low tide or high tide. Observe how the shelled animals behave under these different conditions.

How many different types of barnacles, mussels and tube worms can you find? Watch them feeding when they are covered by water.

Limpets, barnacles and tube worms shelter in shells or tubes, protected from the sun and waves

Wet and dry

The granular limpet lives a bit lower on the shore with the barnacles. It can still be hot there, but the animals can spend more time under water keeping cool. The limpet's conical shell is pale and knobbled and doesn't get as hot as a smooth dark shell would. It fits the rock exactly to give a watertight seal. The waves are stronger at this level and the muscular foot grips the rock firmly when the waves batter the shore. The limpet scrapes the rock bare of seaweeds and then has to wander in search of more food – but it must be able to find its way back to exactly the same place, where its shell fits the rock. Scientists have puzzled over how limpets do this. Usually the limpets follow their slime trail back. However, it has been shown that they can find their way back even if they are lifted and moved a short distance from their trail!

Fixed for life

Acorn barnacles, mussels and reef worms don't risk losing their way home: their shells are glued to the rock. They have to rely on food delivered by the waves. When water flows over the barnacle the plates at the top of the shell open and two fans of fine hairy legs comb the water. Small pieces of food are caught in this net. Tube worms also use feathery fans to filter-feed. Mussels and oysters have two shells that clamp together so that their bodies are safely sealed inside. They open their shells and suck in water from which they filter out little bits of food.

The eggs of these animals hatch into young called larvae that swim in the sea. The larvae are able to move to new areas but it is important that they choose a suitable place to settle and grow into adults as a bad choice, with a poor supply of food, could mean death. They are attracted to places where others of their kind are already living. Once there, they space themselves out so that they do not crowd their neighbours.

Barnacle larva

Barnacle

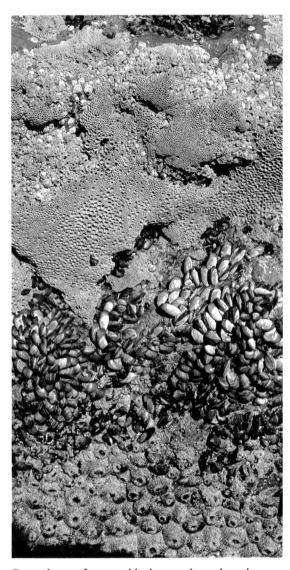

Barnacles, reef worms, black mussels and sandy anemones compete for space

Oystercatchers

Birds known as oystercatchers strut over the rocks on their red legs. They jab limpets off the rocks with their sharp, red beaks and can open and eat mussels. An oystercatcher can gobble up to 5 000 limpets in a year. Where there are many birds leaving few limpets, a rich carpet of seaweeds grows on the rocks.

things to do

Watch oystercatchers through binoculars and try to count how many limpets they eat. Search an area where the birds have been feeding and collect the shells. Which type of shelled animals do they prefer?

An oystercatcher can eat 5 000 limpets in a year

Algae – the basic food source in the ocean

The seaweeds which glisten in rich greens, reds and browns as the tide drops are algae which can form vast underwater gardens to feed and shelter all manner of marine creatures.

Algae (phytoplankton and seaweeds)

Algae are simple plants living in water. Large algae are known as seaweeds and grow along the fringe of the shore attached to rocks. Tiny floating algae are called phytoplankton. Seaweeds and phytoplankton are the food suppliers of the sea, known as primary producers. They make food from water and carbon dioxide gas. They use their green chlorophyll to trap the light energy from the sun and store it as food energy during a process known as photosynthesis. Algae form a very important part of the ocean ecosystem. If you look at the food chain on page 15 you will see that they are at the start of the food chain.

things to do

Break open the two halves of a mussel shell. You will see the threads that glue the shell to the rock and the strong mussel that holds the shells closed. The soft body of the animal is either yellow, orange, red or brown depending on the type of mussel and whether it is male or female. The folded, frilly flaps below the body are the two gills which are used for breathing and feeding. They have fine hairs that collect food from the water and move it to the mouth.

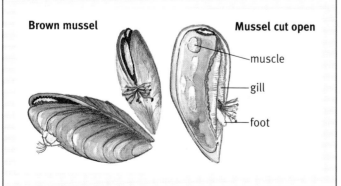

Brown mussel   **Mussel cut open**

— muscle

— gill

— foot

Plankton

Planktonic individuals are tiny and we only see them when there are so many that they colour the waves. If you look at them through a microscope you can see the tiny cells spinning along, driven by hair-like tails. Animal plankton is known as zooplankton and the tiny plants as phytoplankton, although the simplest of these planktonic forms show both animal and plant characteristics and it is sometimes difficult to decide which group they belong to. Zooplankton feed on phytoplankton.

Filter feeders

Many animals are adapted to sieve plankton from the sea for food. They range from the tiny zooplankton, through mussels, sponges and sardines to huge whales and manta rays. Filter feeders usually have fine hairs, feathery tentacles or use their gills to collect plankton. Mussels, oysters and clams make a delicious meal but they are sometimes poisonous because of the way they feed and what they eat. If the water is polluted the mussel itself becomes polluted.

A group of filter feeders including fan worms, red and grey sponges, a sea squirt and a red sea fan. Can you see the tiny shrimp that is not a filter feeder?

Why did 10 million crayfish walk out of the sea?

In 1997 millions of crayfish walked out of the sea and were stranded on the rocks at Elands Bay. They weighed about 2000 tons, which is as much as a whole year's catch for the South African crayfish industry. About 500 tons were rescued and returned to the sea in other areas but the rest were collected and died. Many of the crayfish were small and it will take years for the population to recover. People said it was because of the red tide. Were they poisonous?

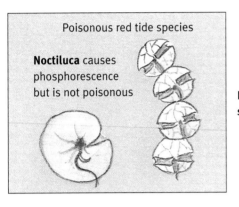

Poisonous red tide species

Noctiluca causes phosphorescence but is not poisonous

Phytoplankton in red tides as seen through a microscope

What is a red tide?

A red tide occurs when the water is so full of phytoplankton it looks as if it has a red scum floating on it. This can sometimes flash with phosphorescent light seen at night. Some types of red tide are poisonous and mussels that feed on them will store the poison for several months. If you eat these mussels they may be poisonous enough to kill you. The Sea Fisheries Research Institute can tell you whether there has been a red tide recently. Poisonous red tides are common only on the west coast. Animals like rock lobsters and perlemoen are not filter feeders and do not become poisonous from the red tide. Birds and most marine animals are not harmed by red tides unless they eat poisoned mussels.

Oxygen shortages cause a 'walk-out'

If the red tide is very thick and there is no wind to blow it off-shore it will die and sink to the bottom and start to rot. Bacteria that cause decay use up all the oxygen in the water. As a result, bottom-dwelling fish and crayfish will suffer from a lack of oxygen. They will move to the surface or edge of the sea to try and find oxygen and so become stranded and die.

Rescuing the crayfish

Crayfish (rock lobsters) stranded at Elands Bay

Seaweeds and herbivores

You will find many different seaweeds growing at the edge of the shore. Compare them with land plants. Seaweeds are quite different because they don't have flowers or seeds, but reproduce using tiny spores. Note how well they are suited to life in the sea.

Seaweeds

Seaweeds anchor themselves to the rocks and can take in water and nutrients through the whole plant surface and have no need for roots. There are green, red and brown seaweeds. They all have green chlorophyll, like land plants, but some have red and brown colouring, which masks the green colour, to help them absorb light in deep blue water.

things to do

Examine and feel the seaweeds and try to work out how their shape and texture are adapted to where they live. Think of both the physical stresses like waves and drying out, as well as the activities of other plants and animals.

Frond shapes in calm water and in waves

A seaweed that grows in calm water is usually large and flat to absorb as much light and nutrients as possible. A seaweed with knobs and small leaves has a greater surface area and can absorb even more light and nutrients than those without. Green sea lettuce can live in changing concentrations of salt, so it is found where streams enter the sea, and in tidal pools which can be diluted by rain or become very salty on a hot day when the water evaporates. Many seaweeds are soft and have split fronds that flow with gentle waves. Where the waves crash onto the rocks you will find tough branching seaweeds or low growing crusts that cling tight.

Flat green and red seaweeds growing in calm water

Hanging wracks live in strong waves

Catching the light

Some plants have air bladders to float them up to the light. The green strap caulerpa is often partly buried by sand. Its green colouring can move to the exposed tips of the plant to collect light, or can go deep inside to avoid sunburn.

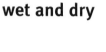

wet and dry

Tide in – swollen jelly-filled deadman's fingers

Tide out – the living skin is wrinkled but not damaged

things to do

Purple laver lives high on the shore and looks like black plastic when dry. Measure a dry plant, then wet it thoroughly and measure it again. It has a jelly layer that swells with water.

Purple laver is edible

Herbivores

Many molluscs, sea urchins and fishes are herbivores (they eat only plants). Winkles, chitons and limpets have flat tongues with rows of teeth. You can see their rasp marks on seaweeds. The perlemoen earshell eats large kelp plants. It lifts up part of its foot and clamps down on pieces of kelp as they are swept under it by the waves, so that it can munch away for hours.

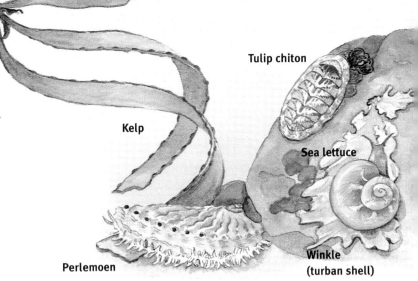

green caulerpa

chalky coralline seaweed

Seaweeds that are hard and chalky or taste unpleasant to discourage herbivores

An experiment

Limpets were kept out of the square on the rocks by a strip of poisonous paint that they could not cross. Seaweeds soon grew in the protected square, providing a sharp contrast to the bare surrounding rock where limpets continued to graze. If people harvest too many limpets the seashore soon becomes over-grown with seaweeds.

Antifouling paint

things to do

Look for the gardens of pear limpets and long-spined limpets.

See how many pear limpets you can find stacked on top of one another. What is the record number of pear limpets you can find in a square metre?

Gardening limpets

The pear limpet lives in the rough waves low on the shore. It can't leave its home scar for fear of being washed away. Instead of scraping the rock bare of all food, it helps a fine red seaweed to grow like a little garden around it. The limpet nibbles only the tops off the seaweed, as if it is mowing a quick-growing lawn, and never uses up its supply of food. Little limpets make their homes on the backs of bigger limpets. On the south coast these successful gardeners form a solid band low on the shore.

The long-spined limpet changes its diet as it grows. Little limpets feed on a brown seaweed that coats the shells of winkles. When they are too big for the winkle they have to make do with a diet of different seaweed, which looks like white paint on the rocks. Eventually, they get big enough to protect a garden of brown, crust-like seaweed and will push away other shells if they try to steal a bite.

Pear limpets and long-spined limpets on their seaweed gardens

Why some shells have holes

If shells protect the soft snail inside, why do some shells have holes? Have a close look at the shells you have collected on the beach. There are two types of shells which always have holes: earshells and keyhole limpets. Others sometimes have holes which have been drilled by predators.

Shells that use holes for breathing

The holes in the keyhole limpet and the earshell are used to direct water currents through the shell. Water flows in through one opening in the shell and brings life-giving oxygen to the gills. It then passes out of another hole in the shell, carrying away waste materials and eggs, flushing them into the sea. In this way the shells solve the problem of separating clean incoming water from the dirty outgoing current.

Keyhole limpets suck water in at the front of their shells. They squirt the stale water through a tube that sticks out of the keyhole in the top of their shells. They usually live low on the shore and often hide under rocks and feed at night. Because they have holes in their shells they cannot survive in the open. In fact, the shell is too small to protect the body. It only covers the gills, and looks like a little cap on the limpet's back. The shell of the mantled keyhole limpet lies under the skin of the slug-like animal.

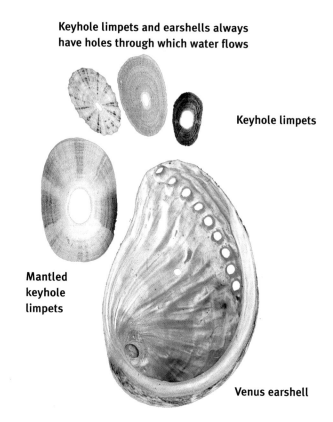

Keyhole limpets and earshells always have holes through which water flows

Keyhole limpets

Mantled keyhole limpets

Venus earshell

The earshell sucks water in at its head. This then flows out through the row of holes along the edge of the shell. As the shell grows, the holes at the back are filled in. The helmet shell, like other whelks, does not have holes in its shell. Instead, it sticks a tube through a groove in the opening of its shell. Water is sucked in through the tube and then passes out at the side of the head.

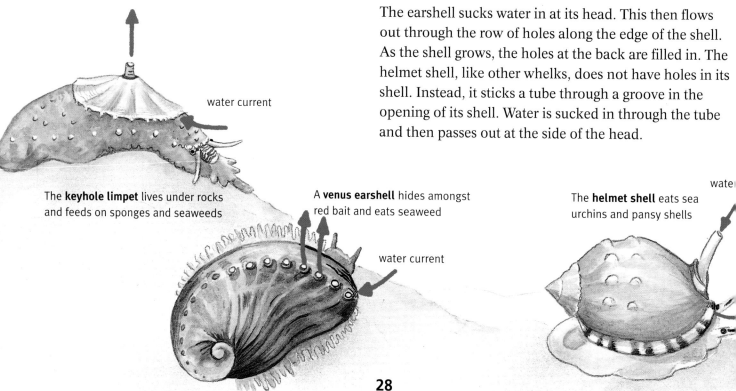

water current

The **keyhole limpet** lives under rocks and feeds on sponges and seaweeds

A **venus earshell** hides amongst red bait and eats seaweed

water current

The **helmet shell** eats sea urchins and pansy shells

wate

28

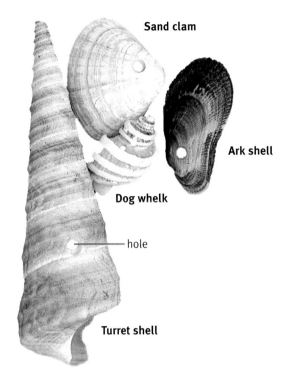

Sand clam

Ark shell

Dog whelk

hole

Turret shell

These shells have been drilled and eaten by whelks – which are carnivorous snails with a coiled shell

Holes drilled by whelks

Holes in other shells are usually a bad sign. They show that the shell may have been killed by a drilling whelk (see page 19G). Whelks eat shells that are fixed to the rock or are not very active. The whelk makes acid that softens the shell of its victim and then drills a neat hole with its tongue. It sticks its long snout through the hole and feasts on the soft living animal inside. Even the giant clam with its pair of thick ridged shells is not safe. A drill hole has been found in a shell which was 50 centimetres long and 2 centimetres thick. The sundial shell selects easier prey and sucks the juices of soft zoanthid anemones.

things to do

Drop some bait into a pool and watch the scavenging whelks attack it.

See if you can find drilling whelks in action. Look amongst limpets, barnacles and mussels. Hold a whelk so that its foot touches a limpet that is covered with water and see what they both do.

Cone shells harpoon their prey

Some shells have venoms that paralyse their prey. The cone shell has loose harpoon-shaped teeth which it jabs into its prey along with some venom. Be careful of cone shells: some of the larger species are fish eaters and are dangerous to humans as well. Others can give a sting like a bee. Most of the small common species, however, feed on marine worms and are no threat to humans.

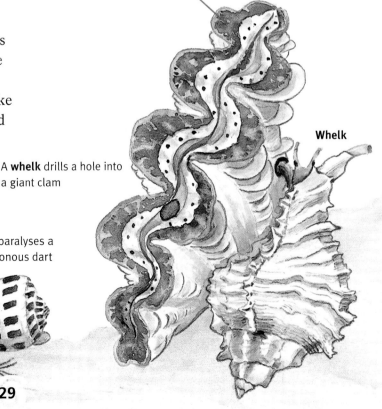

Bright mantle which contains tiny algae that use sunlight to make food for themselves and the **clam**

Whelk

A **whelk** drills a hole into a giant clam

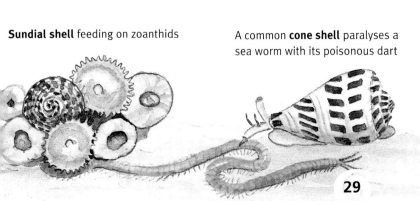

Sundial shell feeding on zoanthids

A common **cone shell** paralyses a sea worm with its poisonous dart

Shells and their enemies

Molluscs have many enemies: oystercatchers jab shells off the rock; seagulls drop mussels from a height to break them open; octopuses, whelks and even the large spiny starfish all feed on molluscs. However, fish and crabs are their worst enemies.

Protection

Some shells run and hide: periwinkles spin and flee from starfishes and whelks, while angel wings can swim backwards by clapping their two shells together. There is a shell that can even burrow into wood to find a safe hiding place. Oysters clamp shut so that they are safe inside their shells. You have to surprise a limpet if you want to knock it off a rock. It takes a force equal to lifting a 100-kilogram weight to budge a large limpet once it has a firm grip. The false limpet is easy to pull off the rocks but it is never eaten by birds or fish or drilled by whelks because its milky slime tastes unpleasant.

things to do

Examine your shells. How are they adapted to avoid being eaten? Find out where they came from and look around for likely enemies.

Many fish swallow shells whole

The sucker fish has a suction pad under its belly so that it can grip the rock. It sneaks up on limpets and pulls them free with its two strong curved teeth. If, however, the shells have spines or knobbles the fish finds them hard to swallow.

things to do

Compare shells from different areas. Which are thicker? How long are the spires? How big are their openings? There are usually more predators in the warmer tropical waters on the east coast than in the cold waters on the west coast. Look at the tropical giant clam and the whelk on page 29 and see their thick, ridged shells.

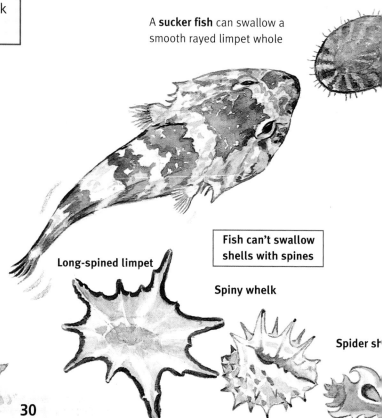

A **sucker fish** can swallow a smooth rayed limpet whole

Fish can't swallow shells with spines

Long-spined limpet

Spiny whelk

Spider sh

Angel wings can swim by clapping their shells together to escape

The **false limpet** has unpleasant slime

Periwinkle escaping from a **whelk**

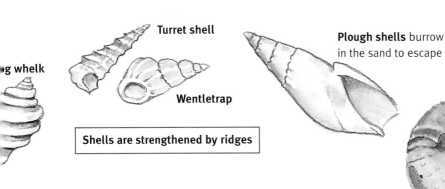

Turret shell

g whelk

Wentletrap

Plough shells burrow
in the sand to escape

Shells are strengthened by ridges

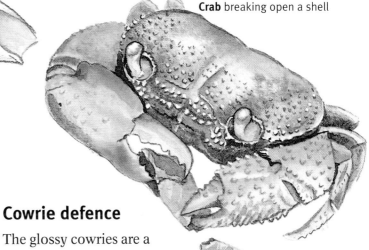

Crab breaking open a shell

Crab attack

Thin shells that have long pointed spires and wide
mouths can easily be gripped and broken by crabs
using their strong nippers. An animal with a thick shell
is more difficult to break open but has a heavier load
to carry. Many shells are ridged or knobbled to make
them stronger without adding too much weight. Some
shells also have short spires and narrow openings to
keep enemies out or have 'doors' to close the opening
against attackers.

The ridged nerita has a better chance than most of
surviving. Its shell is thick and ridged with a flat
spire. The opening has a strong toothed lip. When
the animal pulls into its shell, it closes off the
entrance with its 'door'.

Marginella has a short spire and
narrow mouth to keep crabs out

Turban shell or **alikreukel**
can reach a size of 100mm
when it is about six years old

thick 'door'

Cowrie defence

The glossy cowries are a
delight to any collector and
were used as money in earlier
days. They have many amazing ways of avoiding a
crab attack. Usually, the fleshy mantle of the cowrie
curves up and over the top of the shell. The mantle has
soft, finger-like spines in mottled colours that blend in
beautifully with the seaweeds. It can also have an
unpleasant acid taste. The mantle covering keeps the
shell very smooth and shiny. If the cowrie is in real
danger it can pull back completely into its shell. The
shell has no outer spiral and the mouth is very narrow
and strengthened with toothed lips. It would be as
hard for a crab to break the polished cowrie shell open
as cutting a marble in half with a pair of scissors. Live
cowries are difficult to find because they hide in
crevices, but they are not safe from the octopus, which
can grip the shell with its suckers and bite a hole in it
with its beak. Many different species of cowrie are
found on the east coast of South Africa.

Ridged nerita

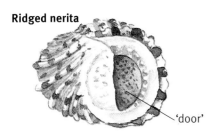

'door'

Polished **cowrie shell** with
narrow mouth and no spire

Tiger cowrie

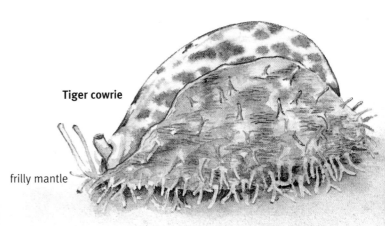

frilly mantle

Rock lobsters and their relatives

Are prawns and rock lobsters your favourite seafood? The rock lobsters (often called crayfish) belong to the animal class called Crustacea, which includes crabs, prawns, shrimps, sand-hoppers and even barnacles. Crustaceans are active creatures and have hard, jointed outer skeletons, two body regions, many legs and two pairs of feelers. When they get too big for their outer skeletons, they have to moult. Because they are so tasty, crustaceans need extra protection to survive.

Why does the zebra shrimp have stripes?

The hermit's house

The hermit crab uses a mollusc shell for a home. It can disappear into the shell and close the opening up with its one enlarged nipper. As it grows, it has to move to a bigger shell. It feels carefully inside the new shell to make sure that it is empty and then, in a flash, transfers its soft tail from the old shell to the new one.

things to do

Place some empty shells near a hermit crab in a pool and see if it will move house.

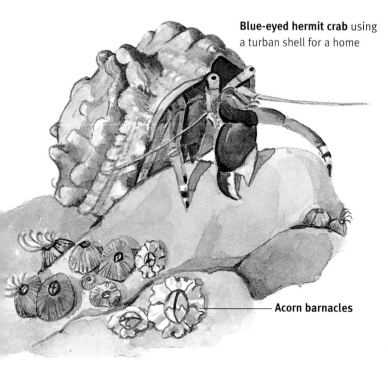

Blue-eyed hermit crab using a turban shell for a home

Acorn barnacles

Barnacles

Barnacles have changed so much to gain extra protection that they hardly look like crustaceans any more. They stand on their heads inside a hard protective shell, and only stick their fine jointed legs out to comb the water for food. Goose barnacles have flexible stalks and drift in the sea attached to anything that floats. Most acorn barnacles are cemented to rocks but some travel around the world attached to the hulls of ships or even to whales. These barnacles slow a ship down because they make its surface rough. Ships have to be scraped and then painted with poisonous paint to stop new barnacle larvae from settling on them.

The **sponge crab** carries a protective cloak of sponge

Cleaner shrimp

Moray eel

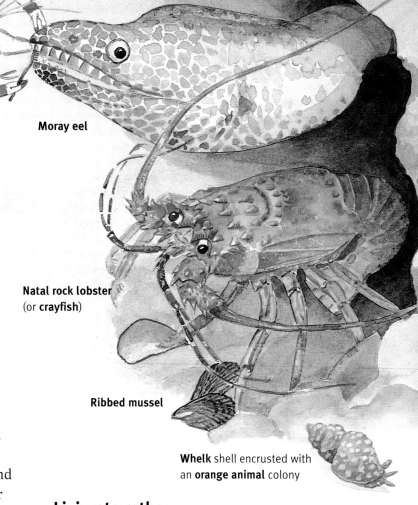

Natal rock lobster
(or **crayfish**)

Ribbed mussel

Whelk shell encrusted with
an **orange animal** colony

conservation

Many people rely on harvesting rock lobsters (crayfish) for their income. The rock lobsters are caught in baited traps or by divers. Fisheries researchers carefully assess the numbers of rock lobsters and calculate how many can be caught and how many must be left to reproduce for the future. It is very important that everyone observes the regulations because being greedy today can lead to poverty tomorrow.

Prawns and shrimps

Swimming prawns and shrimps are active and often change colour to suit their surroundings (see sand shrimp page 15). Sand prawns burrow in lagoons and estuaries. They turn over tons of sand as they sift for food and make spaces in the sand for air and water so that it is a healthy environment for burrowing creatures. Special prawn pumps are used by people to harvest them for bait but a lot of damage can be done to the prawns and other lagoon dwellers as trampling and digging collapses their burrows.

Living together

The dainty cleaner shrimp cleans the teeth and bodies of fish. Its bright colours remind the fish not to eat their useful friend.

Natal rock lobsters and snake-like moray eels often share a hole. When an octopus feels along the ledges looking for a lobster meal, the morays dash out and eat the octopus instead. Rock lobsters feed mainly on mussels and other shells.

Scientists have recently discovered that there is one kind of whelk which is not eaten by the Cape rock lobster. Its shell is encrusted with a red, bumpy, animal colony which probably tastes nasty. In fact, these whelks eat the rock lobsters! The next time you eat a rock lobster, remember that it has moulted 13 times as a larva and is between 7 and 15 years old!

things to do

Look for goose barnacles on the beach after a storm. Place them in water and watch them open and sweep the water with their legs.

things to do

Examine a crustacean skeleton and see how the thin joints allow the parts to move.

The sea stars

Starfish, brittle-stars and feather stars have no heads or eyes, no front or back – it is hard to believe that they are living creatures. They are fascinating animals, full of surprises.

Spiny starfish

Starfish have spiny skins

A starfish has a spiny skin that is hard but can bend. If you look at it through a magnifying glass you will see a mosaic of knobbled plates. These plates are held together by elastic threads. This skeleton grows as the starfish does and so, unlike crabs, a starfish does not have to moult. Seaweeds and barnacles do not grow on starfish because there is a thin layer of skin over the plates. There may also be tiny stalked nippers on the surface of the skin which remove anything that tries to settle there.

'Inside-out' stomachs

If you overturn a starfish you may see a thin bag being tucked away inside the mouth in the centre of the animal. This is the stomach, which the starfish pushes out of the mouth onto its food. The food is dissolved by stomach juices and then taken in.

A spiny carnivore

Most South African starfish feed on fine plant material, but one starfish, the large spiny starfish, is a carnivore. It feeds on red bait and molluscs. It humps over a mussel and pulls the two halves of the shell apart with its tube feet. As one set of tube feet tire so another team takes over until the poor mussel can't keep its shell closed any longer. The starfish then sticks its stomach into the shell and eats the animal.

things to do

Place a large spiny starfish so that it touches a winkle or a limpet in a pool. What do they do? Notice the red sense organ at the tip of each arm.

The tube feet of the starfish end in suckers which grip rocks. Simple tubes on top act as gills

Creeping on tube feet

Starfish usually have five arms beneath which are rows of wriggling tube feet with suckers at their tips. These grip the rocks and move the starfish in any direction. Instead of blood, starfish have sea water running through tubes in their bodies. These tubes are joined to the tube feet, which can be lengthened by having water pumped into them. The sea water enters the tube system through a sieve-plate on the top of the starfish. Starfish can regrow arms that are lost.

Basket star

Brittle-stars

Brittle-stars have long delicate arms joined to a disc in the centre. They are called brittle-stars because their arms break off easily. Some brittle-stars are smooth and scaly but others have many spines. Most starfish and brittle-stars lay eggs that hatch into swimming larvae but the young of some brittle-stars grow in pouches inside their mothers. Brittle-stars often hide under boulders. Their long arms can be seen sticking out from crevices to catch bits of food in the water. The most spectacular brittle-stars are the black-and-white patterned basket stars. The arms of these big starfish have many branches with beautifully curled tips.

Feather stars

Divers often find colourful feather stars with ten or more long feathery arms. They grip rocks with the short hooked arms beneath the body and use feathery arms to collect fine bits of food. Some 350 million years ago the ancestors of feather stars were among the most common sea creatures.

Feather stars

The brittle-star moves by writhing its arms. Its tube feet do not have suckers

Urchins and sea cucumbers

Sea urchins and sea cucumbers are related to the starfish although they look very different. They are all part of the animal group called echinoderms which means hedgehog or spiny skin.

Prickly balls

Live sea urchins are prickly and use their spines for protection, for walking or even digging. Between the urchin's spines there are rows of long, slender tube feet. These grip the rock and often hold pieces of shell and seaweed which they use as a shield against the sun or as camouflage. Little stalked nippers between the spines keep the skin clean and attack predators. Sea urchins have complex jaws with five strong teeth. They eat seaweeds and scrape the young plants off the rocks. If Cape urchins are removed from a kelp forest, three times as many kelp plants grow because the young plants are not being eaten. It is hard to believe that these small prickly creatures can have such a great effect on giant kelps which grow up to 40 metres long.

The sea pumpkin is really the shell of a dead sea urchin

Detail of part of an urchin shell showing the central anus, five holes where the eggs are released and the triangular sieve plate

Urchin shell

Urchin shells, or sea pumpkins, are often found washed up on the shore. The shell is like a jigsaw puzzle of plates joined together. It has rows of small holes for the tube feet and knobs to which the spines are attached. The anus is in the centre. One of the plates forms a sieve through which water flows into the tube system. The water is used to pump up the tube feet. The shell grows with the animal so that it does not have to moult.

Needle urchin are dangerous

Black needle urchins have long, hollow spines. The spines point towards any danger. Great care should be taken not to stand or sit on these pin cushions. If you do, the tips of the hollow spines break off and release venom. The spines cannot be easily pulled out because they are covered with tiny hooks. They can be dissolved with vinegar or dug out with a needle. If they are deep you may need the help of a doctor.

things to do

Watch sea urchins wave their spines at you. Look for their tube feet.

Detail of sea urchin showing the spines, tube feet and minute stalked nippers

Live Cape urchins have solid spines which are not venomous

Sea cucumbers

Sea cucumbers usually lie under rocks or are partly buried in the sand on the ocean floor. They are like tough-skinned sausages. Some are black but many are red, yellow, purple or pink. They collect food with branched tentacles that stick out of the mouth. If they are disturbed, some cucumbers squirt out sticky threads that entangle their enemies. Others will spit out their whole gut as an offering to a fish so that they can escape. They grow a new gut in its place.

things to do

Give a sea cucumber time to expand its tentacles and watch it feeding.

Red-chested sea cucumber

Pansy shell

The pansy shell is like a flat urchin. Short spines are used to dig the animal into the sand where it feeds on fine particles of food. The pansy pattern of holes is where the tube feet stick through the shell.

Pansy shell

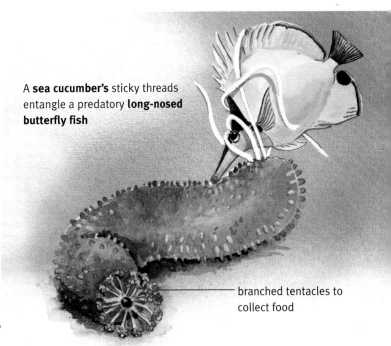

A **sea cucumber's** sticky threads entangle a predatory **long-nosed butterfly fish**

branched tentacles to collect food

37

Rock pools

Sit quietly at the edge of a rocky pool. Examine the rocks. Shake the seaweeds. Drop a few pieces of food into the water. You will be surprised by the number of little creatures living there.

things to do

Float in a pool and look through a pair of goggles.

Shake a bunch of seaweed in a jar of water. The creatures that dart out and swim around can be slowed down by placing them in a refrigerator for a while. Look at them with a magnifying lens.

Look under boulders for hidden animals. Always replace them as they were before.

things to do

Make a seaweed card

Seaweed will keep fresh in a plastic bag for a few hours. Use thin seaweeds to make the most successful cards. Float the seaweed in a bowl of water. Slide a sheet of good drawing paper under the seaweed. Lift the paper carefully so that the seaweed settles on it. Cover the seaweed and card with a piece of cloth and press it between newspaper for a few days until dry. Peel the cloth off carefully. The seaweed will remain stuck to the paper by its own glue. Their beautiful colours will last for years and they have a fungicide that prevents them from becoming mouldy. Marine biologists store their reference collections of seaweeds mounted on cards in this way.

Hide and seek

Can you find the following sea creatures in this rock pool?

1. The zebra fish has black and white stripes.

2. A blacktail is a fish with a black spot on its tail.

3. Strepies are common bait fish that have yellow stripes.

4. The young oculus limpet matches the rock.

5. The tiny clown shrimp is only 1cm long. It grips the seaweed with its back legs and grabs food with its front legs, which are folded like those of a praying mantis.

6. The two flat sea lice are like little cockroaches and swim using their tails.

7. A goby is a fish with a blunt nose and large delicate fins.

8. The pipe fish is long and thin.

9. The shrimp-like amphipod is flattened sideways. It can jump and swim.

10. The sea horse grips seaweed with its tail.

11. The blotcheye soldierfish is red with a black mark above the eye.

12. The spiny seaweed crab hooks bits of seaweed on its back to hide it.

13. Although the sea spider has eight legs, it is not a true spider.

14. Flat worms often live under rocks. They creep or swim.

15. A fan worm sticks out a feathery fan from its tube to collect food.

16. The raggy scorpion fish has sharp, poisonous spines on its back.

17. The brittle starfish has five spiny arms joined to a disc.

Sea slugs

Sea slugs are soft-bodied animals related to snails. Most of them have no shells, but a few have internal shells and the beautiful bubble shell has a very thin shell. They are molluscs (see page 18).

Nude gills

Sea slugs without shells are called nudibranchs, which means 'nude gills'. Their soft bodies have marvellous shapes and colours. Their gills often stick up like bright flexible fingers on their backs, or may look like a ring of feathers. Sea slugs have two feelers on the head with which they taste and smell. How do these soft creatures survive? You will never find them out in the open on dry rocks. They always live underwater and usually hide in seaweeds and sponges or under rocks.

things to do

At low spring tide look among the seaweeds and under rocks for nudibranchs. They are often small but there are many different types. Place them in a pool or jar where you can appreciate their beauty. Watch what other animals do when they meet a sea slug. Remember to return the rock and nudibranch to their original positions.

The delicate bubble shell is unpleasant to eat

Colourful egg ribbon of the black sea slug

The hooded nudibranch creeps up to catch an isopod

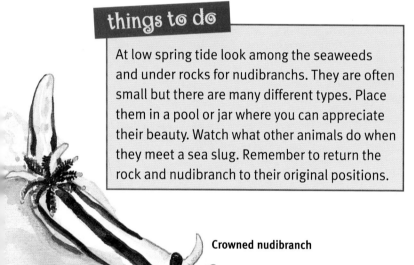

Crowned nudibranch

Spanish dancers can swim

This **nudibranch** has feathery gills

This bright sea slug eats sponges and sea anemones

things to do

Look in tidal swimming pools and lagoons for sea hares. Often you will see their spaghetti-like eggs before you notice the big soft slugs.

A colourful warning

Most nudibranchs are unpleasant to eat because of poisonous chemicals in their skins. A fish has to take only the tiniest nibble to learn to leave them alone in future. Do not add them to a fish tank as the fish might die. Other nudibranchs use 'second-hand' poisons. They feed on anemones or bluebottles that have stinging cells. The stings pass through the body and are stored in the slug's skin, ready for use against enemies (see page 43). These nudibranchs use bright colours to warn off predators.

Camouflage for survival

Some sea slugs have wonderful camouflage. The blue sea swallow, *Glaucus* (see page 9), floats on the ocean. It is blue on top and blends with the sea when seen from above. Underneath it is silver, so from a fish's view it is also invisible. Some sea hares live in sandy lagoons and are a spotted sandy colour. They give off a nasty purple dye if disturbed. Their eggs are like a tangle of yellow string. The sea hare, *Aplysia*, has a thin internal shell.

The sea hare lays eggs that look like spaghetti

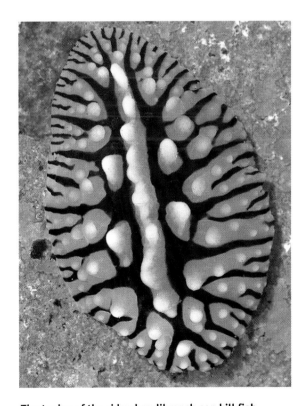
The toxins of the ridged nudibranch can kill fish

Anemones and corals

The anemones and their relatives, corals, sea fans and hydroids, shown on this page, all have stinging cells and belong to the group Cnidaria, which means 'nettle'. They are also related to jellyfish and bluebottles (see pages 8 and 9).

Anemones are animals

Sea anemones look like beautiful soft flowers, but they are animals. If a crushed shell or a small animal lands on an anemone, it is grabbed by sticky tentacles and pushed into the anemone's mouth. The tentacles are covered with microscopic stinging cells. Each cell is like a little sac with a tail coiled inside it. The tail can shoot out and give the prey an injection of venom that paralyses it. Some of these tails coil up and become entangled with the prey. The stings also protect the anemones but are not harmful to people.

Some anemones even attack other anemones that creep into their feeding space. The orange anemone is one of these. It swells up at the base of each tentacle and stings the intruder. Sandy anemones, on the other hand, live closely packed together and the zoanthids on the east coast are even joined together in huge sheets (see page 21).

Sandy anemones of many colours live in dense colonies

Corals

Corals have many different shapes. Their colonies can look like rocks or plants but they are really animals. Coral colonies are supported by hard skeletons of lime (calcium carbonate). The surface of coral has lots of little cups. When alive, each cup contains a small anemone, called a polyp, with tentacles and a mouth leading to a stomach.

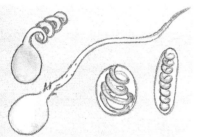

Stinging cells as seen through a microscope

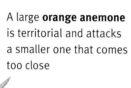

A large **orange anemone** is territorial and attacks a smaller one that comes too close

things to do

Feed an anemone. Place your finger in the tentacles and feel it grab you.

Touch anemone tentacles with a microscope slide and look at the stinging cells under the microscope. You will get more cells if you lick the slide first because the cells are triggered by both touch and the taste of food. Also look at a piece of crushed bluebottle tentacle.

Green zoanthids

Sandy zoanthids

A novel food supply – symbiosis

It is difficult for the crowded coral polyps and zoanthids to catch enough food to survive. They have tiny green plants called algae, living in their bodies. These algae use the waste carbon dioxide and nitrogen from the corals to make food which they share with their coral host. They also help to build the corals' beautiful skeletons. This is an example of symbiosis where a plant and an animal live together for the benefit of both.

Feather hydroids

Delicate feather hydroids house tiny polyps along their branches. They also form buds which break off and float away like tiny jellyfish.

Sea fans and soft corals

The little creatures (polyps) that make up sea fans and soft corals are different from other anemones. They have eight branched tentacles. Soft corals are delicate and they sway gently in the water. They come in many beautiful colours. Red sea fans have a hard red support and can form underwater forests 3 metres in height. When they get this big they must be extremely old because red sea fans only grow a few millimetres a year.

> **Don't be destructive and collect sea fans and corals – they are much more attractive when alive!**

Two delicate feather hydroids growing on a seaweed

The polyps of soft corals have eight feathery tentacles

Detail of red sea fan with white polyps

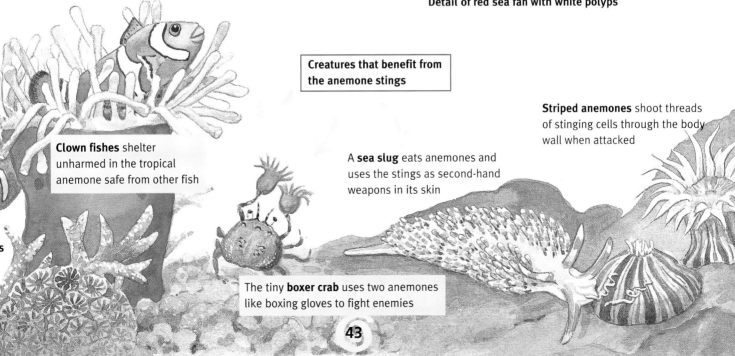

Creatures that benefit from the anemone stings

Clown fishes shelter unharmed in the tropical anemone safe from other fish

A **sea slug** eats anemones and uses the stings as second-hand weapons in its skin

Striped anemones shoot threads of stinging cells through the body wall when attacked

The tiny **boxer crab** uses two anemones like boxing gloves to fight enemies

The kelp forest

A magnificent underwater forest grows along the west coast of South Africa. The 'trees' in this forest are large brown seaweeds known as kelp and can be up to 12 metres tall. They break the force of the waves and provide shelter and food for a community of seaweeds and animals.

Sea bamboo

Red ribbons

Split-fan kelp

A forest reaching for light

Tall kelps form the canopy of shady 'trees'. Fine branching red seaweeds grow on them like ferns and creepers that sway in the waves. Bushy seaweeds make up the understorey plants. On the ocean bed, where there is little wave movement, flat red seaweeds spread out to capture the scarce blue light that filters through the watery forest.

things to do

Visit the Two Oceans Aquarium in Cape Town and view the underwater world of the kelp forest.

Giants and midgets

Kelps shed millions of spores, each smaller than a pin prick. They grow into tiny male and female plants and look like a brown scum on the rocks. Fertilised eggs from these midget plants grow into giant kelps.

things to do

Collect the red ribbon-like seaweed that grows on kelp. Boil it in water to extract a jelly called agar. Add flavouring and let it set in the fridge.

Bladder kelp

Crops grow three times better when liquidised kelp is added to the fertiliser.

Kelp is used in toothpaste, ice cream and many other products.

did you know?

Kelps manufacture food

Like other plants kelps can make simple sugars from water and a gas carbon dioxide, dissolved in the water. They use green chlorophyll to capture the light energy from the sun and store it as food energy in the plant (a process called photosynthesis). The brown and red colouring in certain seaweeds helps to capture the blue light in deep water.

A vast food supply

Kelps grow incredibly fast. They replace their fronds six times a year, and grow like a conveyer belt – adding at the base and wearing away at the tips.

Some animals – perlemoen, limpets, sea urchins, sea lice and strepies – feed directly on the kelp by scraping away at the fronds and sporelings. But many more animals filter tiny bits of kelp from the water. Mussels, red bait, sea cucumbers and sponges feed on the fine kelp soup supplied when the tips of the fronds are worn away by the waves.

They, in turn, become a feast for predators like rock lobsters, octopuses, seals and fish.

things to do

Examine kelp plants that are stranded on the beach. Look for scrape marks where snails have been grazing. Feel the raised patches on the blades where the spores are produced. How many seaweeds, worms and shells are living amongst the branching holdfast that grips the rocks. Why do some kelps have air bladders?

Danger

There are not many dangerous creatures on South Africa's seashores. Even so, you should take a careful look at the animals on this page. Make sure that you will be able to recognise them. Did you notice the stone fish? Watch out for animals that have spines and remember that bright colours often warn that the creature is nasty.

The fireworm and the red and purple sponges have irritant spines

Sponges

Sponges are colonies of simple animals. They are often brightly coloured. Some sponges have tiny glassy needles in their bodies that can cause a skin rash. Water is sieved through the sponge to collect food. Look out for a sponge crab. It grows a piece of sponge on its back to protect and camouflage itself (see page 32).

The fireworm

The fireworm has stiff bristles along its body. These help the worm to grip as it wriggles along. They also give a painful sting if the worm is disturbed. They are found on the east coast.

Sea snake

The sea snake uses its flat black and yellow tail like a flipper for swimming. It cannot move on land. Luckily it is slow to attack but, if you do see one, remember that it is a dangerously venomous snake.

Treatment

Worm bristles and sponge spines can be removed with tweezers or covered with elastoplast for a day or two.

Treatment

An ordinary snake bite kit will not be effective against the bite of a sea snake. Get medical help.

Sea snake

Devil fire fish or **lion fish**
occurs in warm water

Devil fire fish

You will be enchanted if you find a devil fire fish. It is sometimes called a lion fish, because its fins are like the mane of a lion. Its bright stripes and long fins are a warning to all to keep their distance, for along the back of this fish is a row of sharp, venomous spines. The lion fish uses its long fins to herd shrimps and fish into a corner so that it is easy to catch them.

Poisonous puffer

The blaasop or puffer fish can blow itself up. It is often washed up on the beach or hooked by fishers.

If the flesh of the puffer fish is eaten, it is poisonous enough to kill a person

Why are there more dangerous creatures in tropical waters on the east coast than in the colder waters on the west coast?

Treatment

All venomous stings, from bluebottles (see page 8) through to stone fish, can be treated by soaking the wound in very hot water. This breaks down the venom and draws it out of the wound.

When there is an allergic reaction to a sting an antihistamine can be used.

If you are bitten or badly stung by a dangerous animal, see a doctor at once.

Deadly stone fish

The stone fish is the most venomous fish of all. Not only does it contain deadly venom in the sharp spines along its back, but its camouflage is almost perfect. Even when you know where the fish is, it is still hard to see. The stone fish lives in the warm waters of northern KwaZulu-Natal and in coral reefs. It is important to wear shoes when you paddle on a coral reef and it is a good idea to have a stick to poke the area ahead before you step.

Deadly **stone fish**

Fish and fisheries

Most people think of fish in terms of either catching or eating them. When you next see a fish, take a good look at it. Look at its shape and fins and the armour of overlapping scales. If you can catch one, feel how smooth and slippery a fish is.

A proud fisherman throws his haul of snoek ashore

The shape and the fins

Fast swimming fish are torpedo-shaped and use their powerful tails to swim. The two pairs of side-fins act like oars and help them to turn and stop. Fish that swim in and out of caves and reefs usually have larger side-fins.

Senses

Along the side of a fish is a lateral line. This is a sense organ which detects vibrations in the water and helps the fish to navigate even in the dark. Sound travels easily through water and is heard by an internal ear just behind the eye. Inside the fish is a swim-bladder which can be filled with gas to stop the fish from sinking. Sometimes this bladder acts like a drum, increasing sounds and passing them to the internal ear. In the ear a small bone rests on a sensitive pad and helps the fish to balance. Fish do not need eyelids or lashes as their eyes are washed and kept clean by the sea.

In river mouths the water is less salty and only certain fish can live there

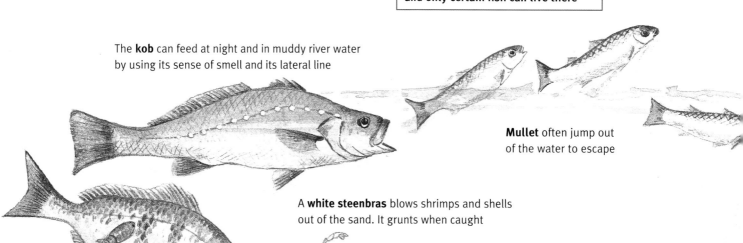

The **kob** can feed at night and in muddy river water by using its sense of smell and its lateral line

Mullet often jump out of the water to escape

A **white steenbras** blows shrimps and shells out of the sand. It grunts when caught

Parasitic **fish lice**

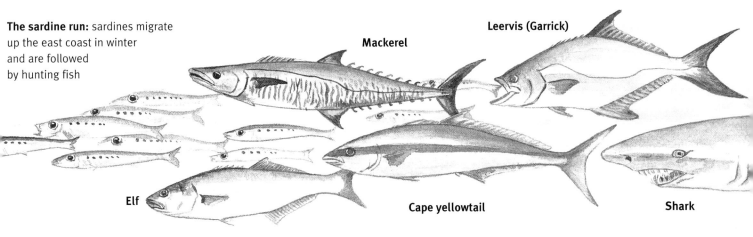

The sardine run: sardines migrate up the east coast in winter and are followed by hunting fish

Mackerel

Leervis (Garrick)

Elf

Cape yellowtail

Shark

Safety in numbers

Fish that swim in the open ocean have nowhere to hide. It is safer for them to swim in schools because predators are confused by the movement of all the fish at once finding it hard to decide which one to catch. A fish also uses less energy when it swims in the slipstream of the fish ahead.

Fishing for schools

Schools of fish are not safe from fishers because they are large enough to be spotted from aeroplanes or located with echo-sounders. The fishing boats then encircle the fish with a large net and the whole shimmering school is dragged on board. It is very important that humans don't catch so many fish that there are not enough left to breed.

things to do

Look at the scales and find the lateral line sense organ on a fish.

Look at the gills of a fish. They are red from the blood that collects oxygen from the water. Sardines have over 100 gill rakers on each gill. They look like combs and net bits of food from the water as it flows between the gills.

Cut open a fish's gut and see what it has been eating.

Boil a fish head and remove all the strangely-shaped bones. Bleach and dry them and stick them onto coloured paper to make attractive pictures.

Collect fish ear bones, especially from the kob, to make jewellery.

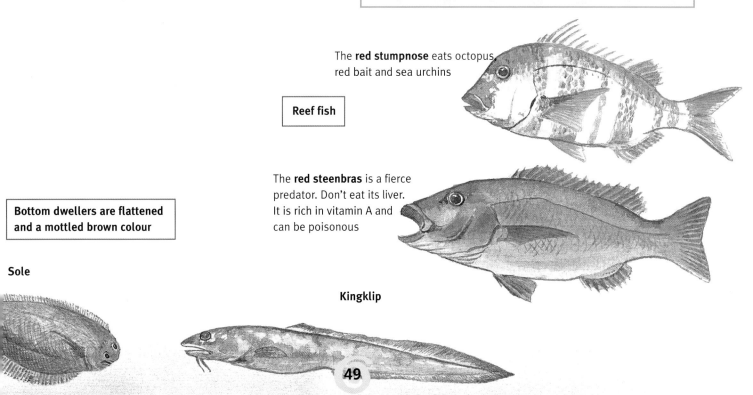

The **red stumpnose** eats octopus, red bait and sea urchins

Reef fish

The **red steenbras** is a fierce predator. Don't eat its liver. It is rich in vitamin A and can be poisonous

Bottom dwellers are flattened and a mottled brown colour

Sole

Kingklip

49

Strange and important fish

There is an amazing variety of fish swimming in the sea. Some fish are of interest because they are very old in origin and show us what the earliest fish were like. Others give an idea of the link between fishes and land vertebrates like frogs and reptiles. Some are adapted to live in surface waters, while others are best suited to life at great depths.

Cowfish

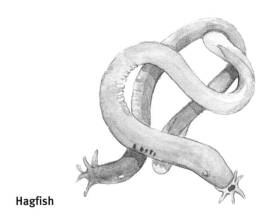

Hagfish

Hagfish – ancient origins

Hagfish use sensory whiskers to feel their way because their eyes are poorly developed and lie under their skin. They are primitive fish, with jawless mouths and no fins or scales, and are thought to be like the very earliest known fish. Many people fear them because they look like snakes but they are harmless. Fishers hate them because they are often caught on fishing lines and produce foul slime for defence. Other fish will not come near bait with hagfish slime on it.

Coelacanth – an important find

In 1938 a strange 2-metre-long fish was caught off the South African coast. This was hailed as the discovery of the century because these fish were thought to have been extinct for 70 million years. Scientists also believe that the first vertebrates to live on land, some 350 million years ago, were creatures rather like coelacanths that could use their stout fins for walking. This exciting discovery was made by Marjory Courtney-Latimer. Professor J L B Smith recognised that it was like the fossil coelacanths. Meanwhile, fishers on the Comoro islands off East Africa were also catching the occasional coelacanth but would throw them back because they were not good to eat. Now that they are considered important, they are in danger of being fished out and need to be protected.

Mudskippers

The mudskippers are little fish that crawl out of the water and hop over the mud of mangrove swamps. Like the coelacanth, they have leg-like fins. They can survive out of water for some time because they store water in their gill chambers. They are a lot like tadpoles.

Mud skippers

The **coelacanth** often swims head down using electric pulses to test the sea floor for food. They have eggs the size of oranges that develop inside the female until the young are born

A **shrimp fish** is almost invisible as it swims, head down, feeding on plankton

Sunfish at the surface

The sunfish basks in surface waters slurping in jellyfish. This weird flat fish is the largest of the bony fish and weighs up to 2 000 kilograms and produces 300 million eggs. It is an intelligent, recently evolved fish. Its tail is reduced to a short rudder used for steering while the long fins paddle it along. Its leathery skin has no scales.

Sunfish

things to do

Try to visit an aquarium or museum to see some of these strange fishes.

Lantern fish can light up

Many deep-water fish have flashing lights. These are used to find prey, confuse predators, and recognise their mates. Lantern fish have many small lights. There are millions of tons of lantern fish in South African waters. They are an important food for snoek, yellowtail, hake and squid, so fishers should try not to net too many of them.

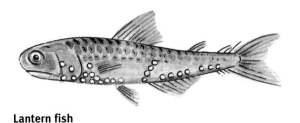

Lantern fish

The male **seahorse** gives birth to many miniature babies

Seahorses

Seahorses are perhaps the most endearing of little fish. They drift through eel grass in lagoons, relying on camouflage for protection. Interestingly, it is the male who becomes pregnant. The female lays her eggs in a pouch on the male's belly, where they hatch and grow. The centimetre-long babies pop out and drift away. Seahorses have a hard armour of fused scales. They are endangered because people collect them for curios and home aquaria.

51

Tropical fish – an explosion of colour

Vivid fish with exotic patterns swim in the sunny waters of tropical reefs and dart among colourful corals and sponges. Their colours are brightest when the fish are active. The black and white clown trigger fish fades to a pale grey when it sleeps.

The **clown trigger fish** can lock its dorsal spine upright so that it can't be pulled out of a rocky nook

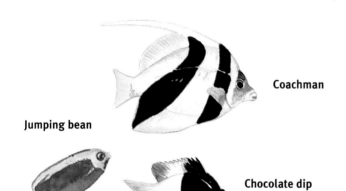

Coachman

Jumping bean

Chocolate dip

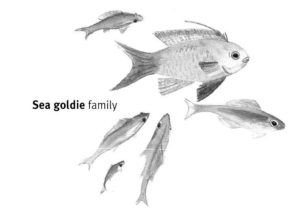

Sea goldie family

Why are they so colourful?

Tropical fish have good colour vision and use their colours to signal and communicate with one another. Their bright colours help to keep them safe from some sharks that cannot see colour. Imagine the fishes' exotic patterns in black and white and you will realise how difficult it is for a shark to make out their true shapes. The fish often have a black stripe that disrupts their outline and conceals the fish's eye, while false eye spots distract predators.

Recognising a mate

The male emperor parrot fish is blue while its mate is red and green allowing instant recognition. They have strong beaks of fused teeth for crushing the coral on which they feed. Sea goldies live in family groups, the females are orange and gold with a blue stripe, while the males are red with a long spine on the back fin. There is only one dominant male but if he dies one of the females can change sex and take his place.

Territorial flags

Tropical fishes map the reef out into territories which they share with mates and young fish. Other fish of the same species that compete for the same type of food are chased off. Their bright bodies are like fighting flags fluttering outside their properties. To make sure there are no mistakes the young emperor angelfish is navy with pale blue circles, while the adult is dark brown with orange stripes (see page 53).

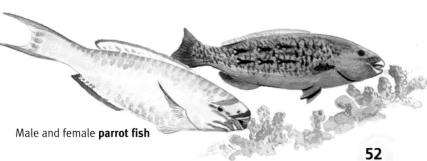

Male and female **parrot fish**

Freckled hawkfish coloured for camouflage

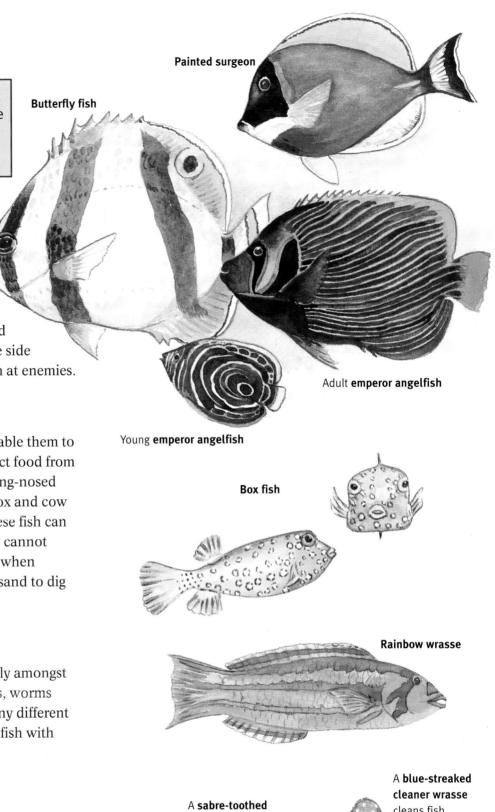

things to do

Visit an aquarium to see some of these tropical fishes.

For a real treat snorkel on a coral reef.

Painted surgeon

Butterfly fish

Adult **emperor angelfish**

Young **emperor angelfish**

Warning of danger

Sometimes distinctive colours and patterns warn that an animal is dangerous. The devil fire fish on page 47 is a good example. The painted surgeon has a razor-sharp spine on the side of its tail, that can be extended to slash at enemies.

Shaped for success

The unusual shapes of tropical fish enable them to move in and out of the coral and collect food from unusual places (see for instance the long-nosed butterfly fish page 37). The scales of box and cow fishes are fused into a stiff armour. These fish can move and turn in tight spaces but they cannot escape quickly and so release poisons when frightened. They squirt water into the sand to dig up their food.

Box fish

Colours for camouflage

The bright rainbow wrasse waits quietly amongst colourful seaweeds and captures crabs, worms and small fish. Rock cods come in many different colours and lurk in caves and capture fish with their big mouths.

Rainbow wrasse

Advertising useful services

The famous blue-streaked cleaner wrasse works unharmed on dangerous fishes, performing an important health service by eating parasites and cleaning wounds. It flutters its fins and does an unusual dance to advertise its cleaning services. The sabre-toothed blenny copies the cleaner fish, but instead of cleaning other fish it snatches a surprise bite!

A **blue-streaked cleaner wrasse** cleans fish

A **sabre-toothed blenny** bites a fish

The **rock cod** starts life as a female and changes to a male when older

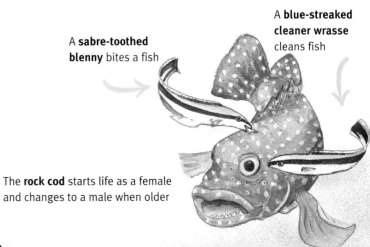

Sharks and rays

There are over 600 different sharks and rays in the ocean. Unlike bony fish they have skeletons of cartilage and their fins cannot be folded up. They don't have scales but a rough skin with little teeth embedded in it. Sharks do not have swim-bladders. Their lateral fins prevent them from nose diving to the bottom and the oil in their large livers gives them buoyancy. They have five gill slits on each side of their bodies. Sharks have ancient origins and have been major predators for over 350 million years.

Zambezi shark

Amazing shapes

Not all sharks are aggressive, fast swimmers. The enormous whale shark, 15 metres long, is harmless and filters plankton from the sea. Catsharks and shysharks are slow swimming reef dwellers, while their flattened relatives the skates, rays and sandsharks lie camouflaged on the sandy sea bed or glide gracefully through the water. They feed by grinding fish and shellfish with their flattened teeth. The gill openings of rays lie underneath and could get clogged with sand but they have an opening behind the eye, the spiracle, where water enters from above to aerate the gills.

Shark births

Rays and most sharks have eggs that hatch and develop inside the mother. The babies are born in shallow water.

Mermaid's purse

Shark eggs

Catsharks, skates and St Joseph sharks lay horny egg cases, known as mermaids' purses, which can sometimes be found washed up on the beach.

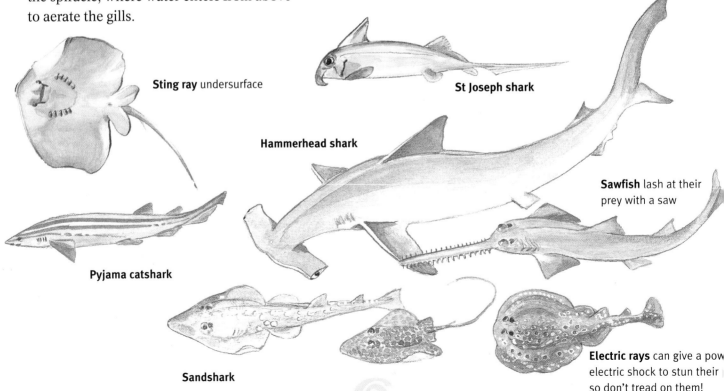

Sting ray undersurface

St Joseph shark

Hammerhead shark

Sawfish lash at their prey with a saw

Pyjama catshark

Sandshark

Electric rays can give a pow[...] electric shock to stun their [...] so don't tread on them!

Efficient predators

Many sharks are streamlined killing machines. They find their prey by using finely tuned senses like eyesight, smell and electricity detecting organs around the nose, and then attack with a burst of speed. Their fearsome jaws have several rows of jagged teeth ready to replace any that are lost. The dangerous Zambezi shark can tolerate freshwater and swims up estuaries sometimes up to 100 kilometres inland. The eyes and nostrils of the hammerhead shark are on the sides of the strange head. It has an exceptional sense of smell and can detect blood several kilometres away.

Great white shark

The great white shark, with its pointed snout and black eyes, is the most dangerous of all sharks. They have even been known to attack boats. South Africa was the first country to protect the great white by law because it is vital to the ocean ecosystem as the top predator and was being killed by trophy hunters.

Great white shark can be over 6 metres long and weigh up to 3000 kilograms

gill slits

Shark attack

Most shark attacks have occurred along the east coast of South Africa. Safety nets are laid in two overlapping rows but do not form a continuous barrier to keep the sharks out. They act more as traps. This is an effective, but not ideal, method because the nets trap not only sharks but also dolphins. The Natal Sharks Board is investigating using electrical barriers instead to keep sharks and bathers apart, and the use of portable electrical devices for surfers and divers.

How to avoid a shark attack

- Sharks are most active at night; don't swim in the evening or in muddy water.
- Avoid wearing sharply contrasting clothing.
- Don't create panic vibrations by splashing like a seal or fish in distress.
- Don't swim when you are bleeding or tie a bag of bleeding fish to your belt.

How to treat a shark victim

Stay calm and call for medical help. Stop the bleeding by pressing on the wound with a wad of material. Lie the victim so that the head is lower than the body. Don't move the victim for 30 minutes to allow the body to recover from the shock. Keep the victim cool and don't give him or her anything to drink.

Sea birds

You can have hours of fun watching birds, especially if you have a pair of binoculars. Most birds can fly. Their bones are hollow but strong and have special air sacs to make them light. The feathers are also light and flexible.

things to do

Watch birds flying. How do they use their wings, tail and feet for take-off and landing? Why do you think most sea birds are black and white?

Fly a kite. This will give you an idea of how seagulls use air currents to stay in the air.

Soaring seagulls

When seagulls fly through the air they use the wind to give them a lift and hardly need to move their wings at all. Seagulls are scavengers and love to follow fishing boats and squabble over the fish guts that are thrown out. They will even grab scraps from a feeding shark! They bob up and down on the water using their webbed feet as paddles. The large black-backed gull, shown on page 11, has a red spot on its yellow bill. The hungry chicks peck this spot to make the adult bring up food for them from its own stomach. Young gulls are a mottled brown colour. The smaller silver gull (above right) has grey and black wings. It is similar to the grey-headed gull on the east coast.

Comical penguins

Jackass penguins are not able to fly. They waddle over the rocks on their short legs and big webbed feet. Yet they are graceful swimmers, darting after fish, using their wings and feet like flippers. The first bird to dive in is often in danger of being caught by a lurking seal. The penguins push and shove one another until one falls in and if he is unharmed the rest join him. They keep together for safety and to herd fish. The short feathers make a warm waterproof coat. Once a year they moult and, as they have to stay ashore until their new feathers have grown, they cannot fish for food. Penguins nest in burrows or among rocks and have one or two fluffy brown chicks.

Jackass penguins only occur in southern Africa. They are a threatened species

A safe nesting place

You may think the nest of these long necked cormorants is in a dangerous spot, perched so high on the rocks. But it is safe from enemies like jackals, mongooses, rats and snakes. It is also easier for the adult birds to take off from a high nest, like launching a hang glider. You can see flocks of these black birds strung across the sky or diving and following a shoal of fish. Their wings are not waterproof and as they get wet the extra weight helps the cormorants dive deeper. After a dive they clamber onto the rocks and hold their wings out to dry in the breeze.

Gannet colonies

You may have seen large white birds plummeting into the sea from a great height. These are the beautiful gannets. They can fly hundreds of kilometres in a day. When they spot a fish they fold back their wings and knife into the water with their sharp beaks. The impact of hitting the water is softened by air cushions at the base of their necks. They have no outside nostrils where the water could rush in. Like most sea birds, gannets nest in colonies on islands safe from predators. Each pair jealously guards its nest which is a hollow in a mound of dried bird droppings known as guano. The parents of the single egg take turns at incubating it with their webbed feet. The chicks are covered in fluffy white down and as they grow become a dark mottled grey.

A runway for take-off

At the side of the gannet colony a strip of land is kept clear. It is used as a runway where the large birds can build up enough speed to lift off. When a bird has to walk through the crowded colony to the runway it is in danger of being pecked. It points its beak to the sky as if to say 'I won't attack, just let me pass'. When a bird lands back at its nest, it bows to its mate and they cross their necks first to one side and then the other. This helps them to recognise each another in these crowded conditions.

conservation in the Cape

At the South African National Foundation for the Conservation of Coastal Birds in Cape Town, birds damaged by oil pollution are cleaned and fed until they can be released. You can visit SANCCOB and help with their conservation work. More than 10 000 penguins were oiled after the Apollo Sea tanker sank in a storm in 1994. Unfortunately, it was only possible to save about half of these birds.

The best place to see Jackass penguins in the wild is at Boulders Beach on the Cape Peninsula. Help to protect this growing colony of penguins.

Bird islands are usually protected to allow the birds to breed undisturbed. But at Lambert's Bay you can cross the harbour breakwater to a small island. Once you have got used to the smell of the guano, you will be fascinated by the birds.

Cormorants nest on high exposed rocks

A gannet points its beak skyward as it walks through the crowded colony. Look for the fluffy white chicks and grey young birds

Marine mammals

Whales, dolphins and seals are the mammals of the sea. They breath air (whales and dolphins do this through blow holes on top of their heads) and give birth to young which are suckled by their mothers.

Ocean giants – whales

Every winter the giants of the ocean visit the coast of South Africa. You may see their huge tails lifting out of the water or hear them puffing air from their blow holes. Whales are not fish, even though they have flippers. They are actually warm-blooded mammals, rather like swimming elephants. They can grow many times bigger than an elephant because the water supports their weight. Beneath their smooth skins is a thick layer of fatty blubber, which helps the whale to float and keeps it warm in the icy water.

The **southern right whale** is the most common whale that visits the coast of South Africa. It is a baleen whale with a smooth throat and no dorsal fin

Although whales breathe air, they can dive hundreds of metres deep and stay under water for up to an hour. During the dive their lungs collapse. The oxygen needed for energy is obtained from their blood and muscles, rather than from air. This prevents whales from ever getting 'the bends' which divers can suffer from if they stay too deep for too long.

Southern right whales come into sheltered bays to mate and give birth. It is exciting to see these big creatures leaping out of the water and landing with a splash as they show off to their mates. The baby whale is born tail first so that it does not drown. It is lifted to the surface by its mother for its first breath. Because it cannot suck underwater, milk is squirted into its mouth from the mother's nipple beneath her belly.

Baleen feeders

You will not see adult whales feeding unless you travel to the icy Antarctic where they eat krill shrimps. Instead of teeth, most whales have horny combs with hairs, hanging from their top jaws. These are called baleen plates. The whale gulps in the water and squirts it out through the baleen hairs which trap the krill. So the largest living creature is a filter feeder! Faster swimming minke and humpback whales have grooved throats.

Bottlenosed dolphins often frolic in the waves and hunt in packs

Toothed whales

The toothed whales include dolphins, square-headed sperm whales, and the black and white killer whale. They use their teeth to capture squid, fish and young seals and swallow them whole.

Echo-location

Whales and dolphins find their way by echo-location. They make high-pitched clicks. The sound waves bounce off solid objects and send echoes back to their ears telling them how close rocks are or how deep the water is. Dolphins and whales are very sociable and communicate with each other with clicks and songs. Not all their sounds can be heard by us but some of them are louder than the roar of a jet and can be heard many kilometres away by other whales.

The Cape fur seal

Seals are rather like swimming dogs. Their legs have become flippers and although they hump and slither clumsily over the rocks, they are swift swimmers. They can stay in the water for days at a time but they must come ashore to mate, give birth and moult. They have a layer of fatty blubber under the skin and a thick coat of fur, for protection and warmth. In October, the males haul themselves onto islands and deserted shores, where they establish territories. The pregnant females arrive next and each gives birth to a squealing, black pup. The pups live off the mothers' rich milk. They play and explore and learn to swim. When they are several months old they can catch their own fish and squid.

Cape fur seals – the largest seal colonies in the world occur on the west coast of southern Africa

Notes to teachers

Active learning

discuss
discover think act

Environmental education themes

Explore the seashore is a dynamic book designed to develop life skills and increase an awareness and appreciation for the marine environment. Each spread is a theme in itself. Important information and recent scientific findings are given to provide a framework for learners' self discovery.

Outcomes based education – developing life skills

Readers are encouraged to go to the beach, look at a fish or visit an aquarium to experience marine life first hand. Practical 'things to do' are suggested to challenge learners to explore by themselves or in groups and expand on the information given.

This book has already been used in schools and proved its worth in increasing general knowledge and developing skills in observation and critical thinking. Learners are encouraged to have responsible attitudes towards maintaining a healthy and sustainable environment. They will become aware of the value of coastal resources for creating jobs and wealth and the importance of conserving the marine resources and being sensitive to cultural issues. The book provides a variety of activities suitable for a cross-curricular approach and could enhance all learning areas of the curriculum 2005 if used with imagination. Many of the critical outcomes of the school curriculum can be achieved by using these themes.

Assessment

Continual assessment can be achieved using project work, oral presentation, group discussions and problem solving exercises.

Some useful references

Two Oceans. A Guide to marine life in Southern Africa
G.M. Branch, C.L. Griffiths, M.L. Branch and L.E. Beckley.
David Philip, Cape Town 1994

*Secrets of the Seas. Illustrated guide to marine life off
southern Africa*
A. I. L. Payne and R. J.M. Crawford (eds). Vlaeberg
Publishers, Cape Town, 1992

Oceans of Life off Southern Africa
A. I. L. Payne and R. J. M. Crawford (eds). Vlaeberg
Publishers, Cape Town, 1989

Living Shores of Southern Africa
G. and M. Branch, Struik, Cape·Town, 1987

Whales, Dolphins and Porpoises
R. Harrison and M. Bryden (eds), Timmins Publishers,
Cape Town, 1988

A guide to the common sea fishes of Southern Africa
R. van der Elst Struik, Cape Town, 1981

Sharks and Rays of Southern Africa
L. J. V. Compagno, Struik, Cape Town, 1991

Some useful contacts

Many of these organisations produce excellent magazines
or teaching aids

Department Environment and Cultural Affairs
(previously Cape Nature Conservation) P/Bag X9086,
Cape Town 8000
Tel. 021 – 483 4227

Department of Environment Affairs and Tourism
P/Bag X447, Pretoria 0001
Tel. 012 – 310 3425

Marine Environmental Education Trust
PO Box 22742 Scarborough 7975
Tel/fax 021 780 1353

Natal Parks Board
PO Box 662, Pietermaritzburg 3200
Tel. 0331 – 471961

National Parks Board
PO Box 7400, Roggebaai 8012
Tel. 021 – 222816

Oceanographic Research Institute (ORI)
PO Box 10712, Marine Parade, Durban 4056
Tel. 031 – 3373536

Port Elizabeth Aquarium
PO Box 13147, Hunewood 6013
Tel. 041 –561051

Sea Fisheries Research Institute
Private Bag X2 Roggebaai 8012
Cape Town 021 - 402 3911

SANCCOB (South African National Foundation
for the Conservation of Coastal Birds) Cape Town,
PO Box 11–116, Bloubergstrand 7443
Tel. 021 – 5576155

South African Museum
PO Box 61, Cape Town 8000
Tel. 021 – 243330

Two Oceans Aquarium and Environmental Education Trust
PO Box 50603, Waterfront, 8002 Cape Town
Tel. 021 – 418 3823

The Dolphin Action and Protection Group
National Save the Whales Campaign
PO Box 22227, Fish Hoek 7975
Tel. 021 – 782 5845

Wildlife Society of Southern Africa
Head Office, PO Box 44344, Linden 2104
Tel. 011 – 486 3294/5

WWF World Wide Fund for Nature
PO Box 456, Stellenbosch 7599
Tel. 021 – 887 2801

Keywords
for *Explore the Seashore of South Africa*

agar a jelly-like substance obtained from red seaweeds and used in food

Agulhas Current the warm current in the Indian Ocean that flows south down the east coast of South Africa

algae (plural of alga) simple, non-flowering water plants; like seaweed and phytoplankton

aquatic growing or living in water

arthropod invertebrate animal with a segmented body, jointed limbs and an external skeleton, e.g. insects, spiders, crabs

bacteria microscopic single-celled organisms without a nucleus, some of which can cause decay or disease

baleen (whalebone) comb-like plates that hang from the top jaw of certain whales, used for filtering food from water

Benguela Current the cold current in the Atlantic Ocean that flows northward along the west coast of South Africa towards the tropics

biological clock the built-in control of rhythmic activities in plants and animals

bladder a sac or membrane that holds various body fluids or air e.g. swim bladder of fish used for buoyancy

buoyant to be able to keep afloat or rise to the top of a liquid or gas

calcium carbonate (limestone, chalk) a hard, white compound found in bones, shells and coral skeletons

camouflage the way in which animals escape notice by blending with their environments

carbohydrate energy-rich organic compound containing carbon, hydrogen and oxygen, e.g. starch, sugar, etc.

carbon dioxide a colourless, odourless gas in air

carnivore an animal that eats other animals

cartilage (gristle) a firm elastic tissue that forms all or part of the vertebrate skeleton

chlorophyll the green pigment found in most plants; responsible for light absorption to provide energy for photosynthesis

colony a group of animals or plants connected together and dependent on one another

coral a group of anemone-like individuals (polyps) which produce a hard limestone skeleton

echo-sounder sounding apparatus for determining the depth of the sea floor beneath a ship by measuring the time taken for an echo to bounce back off the object or shoals of fish

ecology the study of the relationships between organisms and their environment

ecosystem a biological community of interacting organisms and their physical environment

environment physical surroundings and conditions in which all things live

estuary that section of a river that contains salt from the sea. If the mouth of the river is open it experiences tidal flow

evaporate turn from solid or liquid into vapour or mist

feeler (or antenna) a sensory organ found in pairs on the heads of certain animals e.g. crustaceans. Used for smelling and feeling

filter to pass liquid through a porous device (like a sponge) to remove or isolate solid particles (like plankton)

fins appendages used for propulsion and balance in fish and many other aquatic animals

flipper a broadened paddle-like limb used for swimming, e.g. penguin, seal

frond flattened, leaf-like portion of an alga

gill the respiratory organ in fishes and other aquatic animals

grazer any animal that feeds on growing plants

guano the excrement of a sea bird

gut alimentary canal, the food canal in an animal

habitat the natural home of an animal or plant

herbivore an animal that feeds on plants

Indian Ocean the ocean between Africa to the west, and Australia to the east

intertidal between the high tide and low tide levels on the shore

invertebrate an animal with no backbone or spine

larva (plural: larvae) juvenile form of an animal that looks different from the adult

lateral line a line along the side of the body of a fish which detects vibrations and sounds in the water

mammal a warm blooded vertebrate usually with hair or fur. The young develop inside the mother, are born and suckled on milk e.g. humans and whales

migrate move from one place to another

neap tide a tide during half moon when there is least difference between high and low water

nipper a scissor-like claw with moving parts e.g. in a crab

nutrient any substance that provides essential nourishment for the maintenance of life

organism a living individual consisting of a single cell or a many celled plant or animal

oxygen a colourless, tasteless, odourless and gaseous element that occurs naturally in air, water and in many compounds; essential to animal and plant life

parasite an organism living in or on another and benefiting at the expense of the other

phase a distinct stage in the life of a plant or animal

photosynthesis the process by which plants use green chlorophyll to absorb the energy of sunlight and use it to convert carbon dioxide and water into simple sugars for food

plankton the chiefly microscopic organisms that drift in the sea or fresh water; can consist of plants (phytoplankton) and animals (zooplankton)

pollute to contaminate or make filthy (the environment, etc.)

polyp a simple animal with a cup-shaped body and a mouth usually surrounded by tentacles, e.g. anemone

population the inhabitants of a country, place, etc.; the total number of a species e.g. the crayfish population

predator an animal that preys on other animals

primary producer a plant that produces energy-rich food from non-living substances; the first stage in any food chain e.g. seaweeds produce food from water and carbon dioxide

reproduce to produce offspring

respiration the act of breathing; in living organisms, the process involving the release of energy and carbon dioxide from the oxidation of complex organic substances

reserve a place reserved for special use, especially as a habitat for wildlife e.g. nature reserve

saliva juices secreted by glands in the mouth

scales small, thin, bony or horny overlapping plates protecting the skin of fish and reptiles

secrete a process by which substances are produced and discharged for various functions

sedentary stationary or slow moving

shoal a number of fish swimming together

sieve to separate solids or coarse material from liquids or fine particles by passing it through a utensil with a mesh

siphon a tube that allows liquid in or out of an animal e.g. mussel

skeleton a hard internal or external framework that supports the body of an animal; made from bone, cartilage, shell or fibres

spine a backbone or hard, pointed structure

spore reproductive cell of microorganisms and plants that don't have seeds

spring tide a tide occurring at new or full moon when there is the greatest difference between high and low tide

streamlined a form with the least resistance to motion; usually torpedo-shaped

swim-bladder a gas-filled sac in fishes used to maintain buoyancy

tentacle a long, slender, flexible appendage of an animal used for feeling, grasping or moving

territory an area defended by an animal against others of the same species

venom a poisonous fluid in the fangs or sting of an animal; used for defence or to kill prey e.g. snakes, stonefish, bluebottle

vertebrate any animal having a spinal column or backbone e.g. mammals, birds, reptiles, amphibians and fishes

zonation well-defined regions (especially between low and high tide levels) with particular plants, animals and physical features

Index